# THE AI-POWERED SCHOOL

A Hands-on Guide to Integrating ChatGPT and Artificial Intelligence in Schools

Gabriel Rshaid

**The Learnerspace**

# CONTENTS

| | |
|---|---|
| Title Page | |
| Brave New World | 1 |
| The Black Box Effect | 4 |
| \|Applications of AI – Core Subjects | 26 |
| Other applications | 59 |
| Multimedia Expression | 78 |
| Advanced Applications | 89 |
| Ethical and social implications | 104 |
| The future of schools - redefined | 128 |
| AI to the Test: A Case Study | 146 |
| Is it the end… or the beginning? | 168 |
| About The Author | 177 |
| Books By This Author | 179 |

# BRAVE NEW WORLD

*It is difficult to say what is impossible, for the dream of yesterday is the hope of today and the reality of tomorrow.*
Robert H. Goddard, rocket pioneer

I am a self-professed technophile, but also a skeptic regarding the many technologies that have been hailed in recent years as life changing and/or revolutionizing education. It has been a fairly common occurrence in my professional life that colleagues have alerted me about the latest click bait headline proclaiming breakthrough technologies only for me to try to dissuade them from buying into the hype.

Educational technology has been particularly guilty of unethical extrapolations that are now lying in the well populated graveyard of over-hyped software or hardware edtech solutions. In 2022, only a few months ago, Don Hill, a well-known Canadian broadcaster and technology visionary, urged me to check out GPT3, that it would blow my mind. I tried it and, sure enough, it was the best chatbot that I had ever used, but it was just that, a conversational engine but, as I stressed in my talks, being able to converse did not really convey artificial intelligence.

And then came ChatGPT, and the world was forever altered. GPT3.5, the evolution of GPT3, with its unsurpassed natural language processing skills, coupled with a multi-billion token database and a super successful implementation of neural networks and deep learning, resulted in a the first ever generative AI application in history, and one whose characteristics are truly amazing.

ChatGPT, now using GPT4, and a family of generative AI applications that are growing in breadth and depth as I write this, is unlike anything we have seen before. A general-purpose savant and infinitely customizable assistant, this leading exponent of generative AI applications is going to revolutionize the world we live in, and, as usually happens, education first and foremost.

Reactions so far are quite baffling. Despite it being free and relatively easy to access, a lot of people that I know, in many professions, are choosing willful ignorance, mostly out of fear of its immense power. For education, generative AI is a game changer. All that we do in schools can be solved with ChatGPT or other ad hoc AI applications. Educators may choose not to get involved, but students will.

All of a sudden, the many changes in education that were long overdue and that were endlessly discussed in conferences and articles are now urgent instead of wishful thinking. When its use becomes generalized, and it is a mere matter of weeks or months, ChatGPT will force us to finally redefine schools in the face of what becomes by default, at least, a decrepit assessment model.

This impromptu, unforeseen intruder is also a welcome disruption to our traditional modus operandi when it comes to professional learning: there is no time to waste, we will never receive an evidence based guide to successful pedagogical interventions in the application of AI, and the context of schools is in constant flux. We need to learn as we go, a learning paradigm that is much more in tune with a world in exponential change.

This book does not intend anything other than being, as the title indicates, a guide, a shared exploration of the potential and also the risks and ethical impact of the application of AI to education, and life itself. It is my hope that it will serve, as all of us teachers should do, to ignite in readers a passion for learning, in this case, through AI, and to make the most of this turbulent and yet very promising scenario that we are faced with.

There is a saying that serves as a rallying cry for innovators: "We are the ones we've been waiting for". The "we" is not just our collective strength as educators, it is now, and for the future, us and AI, and to deny it is a futile effort. We cannot leave it to the market and tech companies to guide us into how to positively channel the power of AI to improve education. Despite not having a tried and tested step by step guide to successful implementation, we need to, finally, embody what we aspire for in our students: to embrace lifelong learning and confident uncertainty.

# THE BLACK BOX EFFECT

*"With great power comes great responsibility." Spiderman*

For decades already, we have been inadvertent victims of what we can call the "black box effect". Since Google established a de facto supremacy, becoming the undisputed search engine, entire generations have relied on the proverbial search box for anything and everything, from searching the kitchen recipe to trying, perhaps ill advisedly, to discern the cause of symptoms that we feel.

And yet, despite being almost the universal source of all knowledge, very few people know anything about the inner workings of Google, how a search engine is created and developed, its limitations, how search engine results are presented, the infamous "filter bubble" and how it may limit users´ access to reality based on search engine preferences, and a myriad other issues that stem from unrestricted googling.

Even though the use of a tool has become a verb, most users of that tool are blissfully unaware of its underlying mechanisms and how their access to all things learning might be conditioned by them.

The advent of ChatGPT and a, by now, extensive family of other AI related applications elevates the stakes even more. Compared to Google, ChatGPT is not only a couple of orders of magnitude more powerful, it can also process much of what, even at this age and time, was still in the realm of human intelligence. The imminent realization of the promise of Artificial General Intelligence (AGI) renders it almost unequivocal that we need to learn authority, intentionally and scientifically how these systems work so that we become critical users, not just an alphabetization but also a survival skill.

## Learning about AGI

Perhaps the most important point we can make in this book is that it is absolutely essential that all schools include in their curriculums explicit instruction regarding how artificial intelligent works, how it is created, how AGI systems are developed, and what to expect in terms of future developments. Nothing else matters more, as the systems grow in their amazing capabilities it is paramount that students become critical users, and they can only do that by having an in-depth knowledge of how they work, what their scientific basis is, and what to expect from them.

We cannot predict how these systems will continue evolving, but there seems to be a generalized consensus that the foundations for how these systems will continue to grow, almost certainly into superhuman abilities, it is only through a sound conceptual understanding of the inner workings of those systems that we can try to mitigate the almost inevitable dumbing down that they might bring forth.

## How artificial intelligence works

To start with, students need to understand that even though, seemingly overnight, ChatGPT transitioned from being a fancy chatbot proof of concept into an amazing interface for an artificial intelligence that outperforms humans in almost every aspect, AI research and development has actually gone on for decades. As it often happens with great cultural and technological breakthroughs, they become evident all of a sudden but they have been years in the making.

AI research started in the 1940s[1], most notably propelled by pioneers like Alan Turing, and the first very primitive neural network was started as far back as 1943. Early enthusiasm was curbed down by slow development and researchers seemingly hit a wall in terms of improving AI capabilities until two key ideas were developed.

Machine learning involves algorithms that result in AI systems that can learn from data and become progressively better at whatever task they have been designed for. Another significant milestone occurred when researchers started using GPUs (graphic processing units, such as the ones that are embedded in high-end video cards for games) for neural networks, which vastly improved the capabilities of these complex systems that sought to emulate the way the brain worked. This led to what is known as the deep learning revolution, to rapid advancements in areas such as natural language processing, computer vision, and reinforcement learning.

## Key concepts that students need to learn.

The following section includes some of the key concepts, events, and ideas that students need to master in order to comprehend the emerging phenomenon of high-performing AI applications. Needless to say, there is plentiful information on each of these that can brusquely supplement this introduction, and even ChatGPT itself can do a great job of providing clear, concise explanations for each of them.

- **Machine learning** is a branch of artificial intelligence that focuses on developing algorithms that enable computers to learn from and make predictions or decisions based on data. It involves various techniques such as supervised learning, unsupervised learning, and reinforcement learning. Machine learning has widespread applications, including spam filtering, recommendation systems, and self-driving cars.

- **Reinforcement learning** is a type of machine learning where an agent learns to make decisions by interacting with an environment, receiving feedback in the form of rewards or penalties. The goal is to maximize cumulative rewards over time, essentially learning an optimal policy for decision-making. Reinforcement learning is used in various applications, such as robotics, game playing, and resource allocation.
- **Neural networks** are interconnected layers of artificial neurons designed to process and learn from data. They adjust connection weights through training, enabling pattern recognition and decision-making. These networks are a fundamental component of modern AI applications. They basically operate by assigning weights to parameters that are tweaked by the researchers in order to train them and improve recognition.
- **Deep learning** is a subset of machine learning that utilizes artificial neural networks with multiple layers to model complex patterns in data. It excels in tasks such as image recognition, natural language processing, and speech recognition by automatically learning relevant features from raw data.
- **Natural language processing (NLP)** is a subfield of AI that focuses on enabling computers to understand, interpret, and generate human language. It involves techniques such as text analysis, sentiment detection, and machine translation. NLP powers applications like chatbots, voice assistants, and automated content generation. NLP rhythms are at the heart of ChatGPT´s amazing ability to comprehend natural language and generate it seamlessly.

## OpenAI and ChatGPT – A brief history

At the time of this writing, May 2023, and despite the emergence of numerous other AI power apps for every conceivable field and discipline, ChatGPT is still the killer app.

Many of us who enjoy following the latest trends in technology were aware of the development of GPT3, a very advanced chatbot and NLP software that demonstrating amazing capabilities in terms of engaging in a conversation. Even as we were dutifully impressed by how it could be indistinguishable from chatting to a human, thus becoming the first application to comprehensively pass the Turing Test[2], even most of us technophiles regarded GPT3 as little more than a fascinating circus act, for seeing, at the most, that it would greatly enhance personal AI assistance such as Siri.

As the word started to spread about ChatGPT, and we were able to try it out, we were rendered speechless when the newer version, GPT 3.5, married to a multi-billion parameter database, produced results that where almost unbelievable and seemed to deliver, for the first time ever, on the promise of artificial intelligence for the public.

As weeks went by, and the initial impression was reinforced and augmented, it seems, at this point, that OpenAI, the company that owns and developed ChatGPT, may have a decisive advantage in the development of such systems.

Although developments are even more fast-paced than ever, it seems that OpenAI, like Google before it, is poised for global dominance in this hot new market for AI.

As we said before regarding the black box effect in Google, it is more important than ever, especially given that ChatGPT and other applications to come are two orders of magnitude more powerful, at least, than anything we've seen before, that we educators and students themselves learn as much as possible about the company that created it and the stages in the development of the app.

## *OpenAI*

OpenAI, founded in December 2015, is an AI research organization whose mission, as stated in their website (https://openai.com/about), aims to create and promote friendly artificial general intelligence for the benefit of all humanity. Co-founded by Elon Musk, Sam Altman, and other tech leaders, OpenAI initially focused on research collaborations and the development of open-source AI tools. In 2019, OpenAI transitioned to a capped-profit model, which basically entails that it becomes a for-profit company, but with a limit to how much investors can make. After that limit is reached, all other profits are plowed back into the nonprofit arm of the company.

OpenAI has since made significant advancements in AI research, such as GPT-3 and DALL-E, and AI-based image generation system, while still addressing the global challenges associated with AGI.

They receive funding from a mix of private investors, philanthropic contributions, and its own revenue-generating AI products and services. Initial investors include tech leaders like Elon Musk and Sam Altman, as well as organizations like Y Combinator. The transition to a capped-profit model in 2019 also paved the way for additional investment while maintaining a focus on its mission.

Microsoft has been a significant partner and investor in OpenAI, providing resources and support for the organization. In 2019, Microsoft announced a $1 billion investment in OpenAI to collaborate on AI research and development, including the creation of AI supercomputing technologies.

## *ChatGPT*

ChatGPT, developed by OpenAI, is an advanced language model based on the GPT architecture.

GPT stands for "Generative Pre-trained Transformer." The name highlights three key aspects of the model: it is "generative" because it can generate text, "pre-trained" because it learns from a large dataset before being fine-tuned for specific tasks, and "transformer" refers to the underlying architecture used in the model, which is based on the Transformer, a neural network architecture introduced by Vaswani et al. in 2017.[3]

It is trained using a process called unsupervised learning, where the model learns from large amounts of text data, such as books, articles, and websites. The training process involves predicting the next word in a sentence, enabling the model to capture the structure and patterns of human language. Fine-tuning is done using a smaller, curated dataset with reinforcement learning from human feedback, which helps adapt the model for specific tasks or conversational abilities. With each iteration of the GPT series, improvements in model architecture, training data, and techniques lead to more powerful and capable language models.

ChatGPT learns from a diverse dataset containing text from sources such as books, articles, and websites, which spans a wide range of topics and domains. This dataset is constructed by collecting and filtering publicly available text data from the internet. However, the model's knowledge is limited to the information present in its training data, with a cutoff at around September 2021.

It is important to note that while ChatGPT can generate impressively human-like text, it doesn't understand the text in the way humans do. It is just predicting what comes next in a sequence based on patterns it learned during training.

## Biases in language models

Since the early days of the development of neural networks, the learning a language models, researchers found that there was a major issue, that of biases, which needs to be understood in the context of learning about AI.

Early language models for AI, such as word2vec, GloVe, and early versions of GPT, often suffered from biases that stemmed from the data they were trained on. These models learned from large text corpora, which inevitably contained biases present in human-written text, and that reflected existing societal biases in their respective contexts, as is inevitable with any real world data used for training purposes in AI.[4]

Consequently, the biases in the training data were inherited by the models, leading to biased outputs. Some examples of biases and their corrections in early language models:

**Gender bias:** Early language models tended to associate certain occupations, qualities, or activities with specific genders. For example, they might have associated "nurse" with female pronouns and "engineer" with male pronouns. To correct this, researchers developed methods such as debiasing word embeddings by equalizing gender-neutral words across male and female dimensions or by neutralizing gender-specific words so that they don't exhibit gender bias.

**Racial and ethnic bias:** Early models could associate certain racial or ethnic groups with stereotypes or negative sentiments. For instance, a model might have associated a specific ethnicity with crime or poverty. To address this, researchers designed techniques to measure and reduce these biases in word embeddings and other model components.

Some of these biases were addressed by what is known as counterfactual data augmentation, a method used to make AI models less biased. It involves adding new examples to the training data by changing specific words related to a person's identity, such as their race, gender, or ethnicity. This helps the model learn that these identity terms should not affect its understanding or predictions, ultimately leading to fairer and less biased outcomes.

As AI models have evolved, researchers continue to develop more sophisticated techniques for addressing biases, such as reinforcement learning from human feedback, which allows for iterative fine-tuning of models in collaboration with human reviewers to minimize biases and improve overall model performance.

Addressing biases in language models like ChatGPT requires a combination of techniques, including reinforcement learning from human feedback (RLHF) and careful fine-tuning. To mitigate biases, especially with regards to sensitive topics like gender, the training process involves an iterative procedure with human reviewers who follow guidelines provided by the developers. These guidelines emphasize avoiding biases, favoring one group over another, or taking a position on controversial topics.

## What we need to know and teach our students

All of the above leads us to formulate certain conclusions, some of which are temporary, valid at this stage of development, but that are, nonetheless, instrumental towards a better understanding of AI related tools for education, their limitations and potential future developments.

- **It is a closed knowledge database**. This is probably the most important conclusion to be formulated and understood regarding ChatGPT. OpenAI has invested enormous amounts of time and money in the development of a knowledge base that, coupled with a superpowerful GPT 4, the latest version, produces amazing results that dazzle us in their scope, reach and depth. It is absolutely essential to know that the database on which ChatGPT bases its answers has a cutoff date of September 2021, and that, albeit being almost all-encompassing in the knowledge it stores, is finite and limited. This implies that, at least for the time being, and it will surely be successively updated, anything that happened after September 2021 is completely ignored by ChatGPT.

Also, and as far-reaching as it may be, whatever did not bring the cut into the knowledge base for ChatGPT is not part of the reality that it bases itself on. This initial version is not organic and dynamic, it does not update itself continuously as new content is generated on the Internet, so in terms of current events and any other discovery or new knowledge, ChatGPT is blissfully ignorant.

- **Some applications are already tapping into the real world Internet**. Despite the previous point, there are already many applications that can utilize GPT4 on live Internet, such as, for example, those that can transcribe and summarize YouTube videos, searching for and summarizing current trends about a certain Google search, or performing analysis and summarization of live websites. There are also plugins that extend ChatGPT's capabilities to other areas. Several of these applications, including the Microsoft Bing search engine, allow ChatGPT to access the internet and can, among other things, summarize videos, enter websites, etc. While this extends ChatGPT's knowledge base to the internet, it is on demand, meaning one must ask it to reference a particular search or access a certain site to be able to incorporate that information into the natural language features of GPT-4. However, the process is slower and does not do it with the comprehension or speed of what it summarizes in its database. The current plus multimodal version already does this automatically, but only accesses certain sites, limiting its understanding.

- **The system is never going to be 100% devoid of errors**. Even as the latest version (4) vastly improves as compared to its predecessor (3.5), and it is logically expected that succeeding versions will increase their reliability and accuracy, the system will never be foolproof or 100% devoid of errors.

ChatGPT can sometimes hallucinate, or generate information that isn't accurate or based on facts, because it learns from a vast range of text data, which can include false or misleading information. Additionally, during the text generation process, the model might combine various pieces of knowledge in a way that results in an incorrect output. The nature of neural networks and their probabilistic approach to generating text also contributes to occasional hallucinations.

This implies that, especially in the context of education, any output from ChatGPT and future versions needs to be monitored and supervised by teachers. These preclude its indiscriminate use, for example, for some social emotional learning activities or its use by his younger children in various contexts.

- **It is a designed model and not organic**. Even though the unfathomable volume of information contained in the ChatGPT knowledge base gives the illusion of it being unlimited and organic, it is human made, and decisions of be made about what data to include, which biases to correct and how to correct them, and the human reinforcement component inevitably adds an imperceptible but existing layer of subjectivity. In that respect, ChatGPT is more like a massive encyclopedia than the Internet.

- **Extremely sensitive to prompts**. ChatGPT is absolutely dependent on human prompts, to a far greater extent than Google, to which we gradually got used to, in terms of perfecting and refining our search queries. This is so much so that prompt engineering has fast become a new and much in demand profession, individuals who are able to generate prompts that extract relevant information from ChatGPT and provide that service to other people and companies. ChatGPT has taken to another level the old adage of "Garbage in, garbage out", which used to refer to how computers could only output relevant information if they were adequately programmed to do so.

In the case of ChatGPT, as anybody who has attempted to use can readily attest, the accuracy and relevance of the information is contingent on the user´s contextual knowledge of what they want out of the system and their skill at producing detailed, specific prompts that the system can interact with.

- **Plugins**: From the plus version and GPT-4 onwards, among other features that we will analyze in detail later, ChatGPT incorporates the use of plugins. These are ad hoc tools developed by companies, firms, and organizations that provide detailed searches oriented to specific themes. By entering the plugin store, accessible from the paid version of ChatGPT and included in the subscription price, there are literally thousands of plugins. Some are more effective than others, covering diverse areas such as transportation, food, health, PDF reading, site access, academic research, and a long list of all kinds of thematic areas, including some more trivial or entertainment ones. In this regard, we recommend, since the horizon and breadth of plugins is enormous, to visit internet portals that regularly evaluate these plugins to recommend the best ones in each area, even giving examples of their use.

## Its implications on schooling

In later sections, we will discuss, in-depth, some of the ethical and social implications of the rapid advancement of AI and the family of related applications, and more specifically on education, but it still makes sense to conclude this first chapter with an initial analysis of how much this will affect teaching and learning at schools.

Even though it is impossible to predict what the ultimate

impact of ChatGPT, other AI applications, and future developments will actually have on schools, we already know that ChatGPT and all that is to come are literal game changers when it comes to education. This is not just another technological development, it is a point of inflection not only in the history of learning but also for humanity as a whole.

As mentioned earlier, it is of fundamental importance that students are aware of some of the risks, pitfalls and implications of the development of these very powerful tools, and the we will analyze these in extensive detail with a view to generate these discussions and reflections with students themselves. But let us understand that education has changed irreversibly, that nothing will ever be the same again.

In the words of Tom Friedman, who, many years ago, in his book "Thank You for Being Late: An Optimist's Guide to Thriving in the Age of Accelerations"[5] predicted not only the rise of intelligence assistants, but also characterized some innovations as more than disruptions, he called them dislocations, and that is what is happening in the world or education.

When everything is upturned, we are facing a lot more than a disruption. In the few months that have transpired since the generalized deployment of ChatGPT and this incipient AI revolution, I have spoken to numerous school leaders in various contexts about how much it will impact education. And I've heard comparisons to the calculator, and how it did not end the teaching of math, or the development of the Internet and the smart phone, innovations that, despite their immense power, have not fundamentally altered the grammar of schools.

Even though this maybe says more about the rigidity of schools than the extent of the innovations, ChatGPT and AI applications are very different from anything we've seen before. To start with, even though, for example, the Internet on the smart phone developed exponentially in their use in potency in the lapse of a few years, that period was measured in years, and, albeit taking the world by force, it did provide all actors in the system with at least a little time to get used to these new technologies and their applications.

This is most definitely not the case with ChatGPT. In just a few weeks, and right out of the box, ChatGPT has immediately displayed amazing capabilities and moved the cognitive scale at least two orders of magnitude in the blink of an eye, taking everybody by surprise, even their creators, who have manifested their own amazement at how well it worked.

ChatGPT is more like the invention of fire, a decisive and, even if not serendipitous, almost accidental discovery in terms of the actual scope of its application. We need to come to terms with that fear-originated blissful ignorance, as is happening in many a school and to many school leaders, is not an option, since we may choose, overwhelmed by the complexity of it all, to defer its application in the vain hope that it will be another passing fad or that somebody would put a stop to it, but students will not, and they don't need our permission to hack what is, through our own fault, a very vulnerable school system.

## Summary

- The "black box effect" refers to the lack of understanding of how search engines like Google work and how they shape users' access to information.
- It is crucial for schools to teach explicit instruction on artificial intelligence (AI) and its workings, including the development of AI systems and their limitations.
- Students should learn key concepts such as machine learning, reinforcement learning, neural networks, deep learning, and natural language processing to comprehend high-performing AI applications.
- OpenAI is an AI research organization focused on creating and promoting friendly artificial general intelligence. It has made significant advancements in AI research, including

the development of GPT-3.
- ChatGPT, developed by OpenAI, is an advanced language model based on the GPT architecture. It is trained on a diverse dataset, but biases in language models have been a concern that researchers are actively addressing.
- ChatGPT has a closed knowledge database with a cutoff date of September 2021, and its information is finite and limited. Anything that happened after that date is unknown to ChatGPT.
- ChatGPT is a human-made model with inherent biases and subjectivity. Prompt engineering is crucial for accurate and relevant outputs.
- The impact of AI applications like ChatGPT on education is significant and irreversible. It represents a point of inflection and a game-changer in the history of learning, requiring students to be aware of the risks and implications. It is a dislocation rather than a disruption, fundamentally altering the grammar of schools.

**Prompts and suggested activities for ChatGPT**

At the end of each chapter, we will be providing a series of prompts and activities to engage ChatGPT or any other advanced AI chatbot in engaging learning activities related to the topics covered.

---

The "Black Box Effect", Google, ChatGPT and the need to learn its inner workings.
- Explain how a search engine like Google finds *its* search results.
- To what extent does it customize search results based on users´ prior browsing history and/or preferences?
- What is the filter bubble and how does it affect

users' experience?

Understanding How AI Works

- Using a non-computer based example, explain in simple terms how machine learning works.
- Explain in very simple terms what a neural network is.
- Provide a concrete example of how a neural network processes information.
- Explain in very simple terms how deep learning works.
- Provide a simple example of how deep learning can process information.
- We will use tic-tac-toe, one of the simplest games there are, to understand how systems evolved to the current state of the art applications:
    - Using the example of how to play tic-tac-toe, explain in very simple terms how machine learning would be applied to the process.
    - Now do the same but with a neural network.
    - In simple terms, explain how the system be improved via deep learning.
    - Now, in simple terms, give an example of how human reinforcement can make it even better

The Role of OpenAI and ChatGPT

- Tell me the history of OpenAI
- What is its vision for the development of Artificial General Intelligence?
- Where does it get its funding from?
- What is the role of Microsoft in OpenAI?
- Explain the limits to the profits for investors.
- What data set is ChatGPT trained on?
- When will it be updated?

- Why does ChatGPT incur in hallucinations?
- Will it ever be error-free?
- Starting from the prompt, explain in the simplest possible terms each step that ChatGPT takes in order to arrive at its answer.

Addressing Biases in AI

- Explain, in simple terms, why, unless corrected, AI systems trained on large data sets include biases.
- Give examples of such biases.
- Using the same example, explain in concrete terms how the system would be debiased.
- Who decides the set of values upon which an AI system is debiased?
- In very simple terms, explain why current state-of-the-art AI systems are opaque and sometimes even the programmers don't know how decisions are made.
- Is this a risk for future development of AI?
- Have countries legislated the use of algorithmic decisions?
- Should people have the right to an explanation when an algorithmic decision is being made that affects them?

The Impact of AI on Education:

- Give examples and concrete suggestions about how ChatGPT can be used for learning in the school context.
- How do you think schools will evolve when everybody uses ChatGPT and other generative AI systems?

The Future of AI:

- What are foreseeable future developments for AI?
- Can they truly develop superhuman abilities?

## *Sample activity*

### Lesson Plan: Understanding and Correcting Biases in Large Data Sets

Grade Level: High School

Learning Objectives:

- Understand what bias in data is.
- Learn to identify potential sources of bias in data collection.
- Analyze data for biases.
- Develop a set of values to guide in debiasing the system.
- Apply methods to correct identified biases.

Lesson Procedure:

Activity 1: Collecting Potentially Biased Data

1. Divide the students into small groups. Each group will identify a topic of interest (preferably something that can be surveyed within the school community) and develop a survey questionnaire to collect data. Encourage them to think of biases that may occur in their data collection process.
2. Once the questionnaire is developed, each group will survey a sample of the school population (e.g., classmates, teachers, other students) and record the responses.
3. Students will then transfer their collected data into a spreadsheet, learning how to effectively tabulate data.

Here are some examples of possible such surveys and possible biases:

Example 1: School Lunch Survey

A survey could be conducted to determine student satisfaction with the school lunch program. Potential questions might include "How often do you eat school lunch?" and "Rate your satisfaction with the school lunch program".

Potential biases include:
- Selection bias: Students who feel strongly about the school lunch program (either positively or negatively) might be more likely to respond, skewing the results.
- Response bias: The way questions are phrased could lead students to respond a certain way. For example, asking "Why don't you like the school lunch?" assumes the student doesn't like it, which could influence their response.

Example 2: Extracurricular Activity Participation Survey

This survey could ask about student participation in and attitudes towards extracurricular activities. Questions might include "What extracurricular activities do you participate in?" and "What barriers, if any, do you face in participating in extracurricular activities?"

Potential biases include:
- Selection bias: Students who are heavily involved in extracurricular activities might be more likely to respond, skewing the results towards high involvement.
- Non-response bias: Students who do not participate in any activities may be less likely to respond, which could underrepresent the number of students facing barriers to participation.

Example 3: School Climate Survey

This survey would aim to measure student perceptions of the school climate, including safety, relationships with teachers, and peer-to-peer interactions. Questions could include "Do you feel safe at school?" or "How would you describe your relationship with your teachers?"

Potential biases include:
- Response bias: The phrasing of questions might

lead students to respond in a certain way. For example, a question like "Do you feel bullied at school?" might not capture students who don't recognize their experiences as bullying.

- Confirmation bias: Students who have preconceived opinions about the school climate might answer questions in ways that confirm their beliefs, rather than reflecting their actual experiences.

Activity 2: Identifying Biases

1. Introduce the concept of biases in data sets. Provide examples of common types of biases, such as selection bias, confirmation bias, and non-response bias.
2. Have each group analyze their data to identify potential biases. What types of people responded more or less? Are there any questions that might have been leading? Did they sample the population fairly?

Activity 3: Developing Values to Debias the System

1. Engage the class in a discussion about ethics in data collection and how biases can be mitigated.
2. Have each group discuss and write down a set of values that will guide their debiasing process. The values can include fairness, objectivity, transparency, etc.

Activity 4: Correcting the Biases

Preparation

1. Begin the activity by revisiting the concept of biases and the potential harm they can introduce into data analysis and decision-making. Discuss the importance of mitigating these biases to ensure the integrity of the data analysis.
2. Introduce the concept of bias correction and discuss

the primary methods that can be used to reduce bias, such as data transformation, stratification, weighting, or adjusting for confounding variables.

Weighting Responses

3. Teach students the concept of weighting responses, a technique often used in survey analysis to correct for non-response or selection bias. Explain how this can adjust for certain groups being over- or underrepresented in the data. For example, if fewer seniors than freshmen answered the survey, each senior's response might be given more weight.
4. Guide students to create weights for their data based on the actual demographics of the school population and apply these weights in their spreadsheet.

Adjusting Sample Selection

5. Next, discuss the concept of adjusting the sample selection. Explain that if certain groups are underrepresented in the data, additional data may need to be collected from these groups to reduce bias.
6. Have students examine their own data to see if additional data collection might be necessary. If it is not possible to collect more data, students should discuss how they would adjust their sample if given the opportunity.

Redesigning Questions

7. Finally, discuss how biases can arise from the design of the questions themselves. These could be leading questions, complex questions, or questions with a limited set of response options.
8. Have students examine their survey questions for potential biases and discuss how they might redesign these questions to reduce bias. Students can then revise their questions in the survey tool and discuss the potential impacts these changes would have had on

their data.

Reflection

9. To conclude the activity, ask students to reflect on how these bias correction techniques affected their data. Did their results change significantly? Did any patterns emerge or disappear?
10. Lead a discussion on the importance of bias correction not just in school projects, but in real-world data analysis. Discuss how uncorrected biases might affect decisions made based on data, and the ethical implications of this. ---

Reflection and Discussion Questions:

1. How did your group's data collection method introduce bias?
2. What types of bias were present in your data?
3. How did you correct these biases, and how did it affect your results?
4. Why is it important to be aware of and correct biases in data?
5. How do you think bias in data affects real-world systems?

# |APPLICATIONS OF AI – CORE SUBJECTS

Almost nobody saw it coming. As we have said repeatedly before, even the founders and developers of ChatGPT were stunned by the amazing capabilities displayed by the system as it was deployed and users worldwide started to find all kinds of applications for their amazing features. The very nature of neural networks made it not impossible that the system outperformed even its wildest expectations.

As it usually happens with any technological developments, education is both the most impacted field, as well as being the one who takes longer to catch up, fully incorporate and leverage the potential of these applications.

After just a few months of this sudden coming-of-age of AI, it is as self-evident as it is intriguing that the impact of AI in education will be both decisive and irreversible. As with many of the technological innovations that have radically changed the way we learn and live, whatever our value judgment on the potential impact of these new technologies, they are here to stay, they are driven by forces that are clearly outside our power to stop or even thwart, and we educators should better make the best possible use of them since there will be nobody other than ourselves to try to harness their power for learning.

And we cannot wait for a step-by-step guide or an ad hoc AI powered pedagogy, as habituated as we may be to be cautious and expect safe, incremental interventions in terms of any changes we make to our teaching and learning practice. Imperfect as it might be, teachers need to use and help students discern what these AI powered applications can be used for and how they can greatly help their learning.

## The dark side

Before engaging fully in how best to try to apply these very powerful tools to teaching and learning, rather to learning mostly, we need to identify some of the real risks involved, so that these implementations can attempt to mitigate them – as we shall see, some of the risks are real and almost impossible to evade – and focus on the many positives that they bring forth.

Let me clarify that the analysis that ensues is based on the current framework for schooling, not necessarily in terms of the traditional model, but with reference to the cognitive skills, learning and developmental progression that is universally accepted as being the logical path to gaining high order cognitive and thinking skills. We will leave for later in the book a deeper philosophical discussion of which skills may be rendered obsolete in the post AI world and what the opportunity cost to learning them will be.

Some of the risks that can already be identified are:

- **Inhibiting of some cognitive skills**. The excessive reliance on ChatGPT to explain, breakdown, analyze, at the same time that it can be a very meaningful help for students to learn better, it may very well also result in slower development or even in the non-acquisition of certain cognitive skills that are derived from the mental processes involved in having to approach learning from a blank slate.
- **Dependence on AI**. There is consensus as to that some of the most important goals of education, in a world full of opportunities, is to have students learn to self-manage their learning process. Inasmuch as AI can be a

super powerful tool to aid and even empower learners, it remains to be seen whether the continued reliance on AI for the learning process may stifle some of the very higher order thinking skills needed to make full use of it. From generation of prompts to critically analyzing and modifying AI generated content, the skills required to fully take advantage of generative AI involve higher order skills, even when it comes to discerning what the AI can do. Users who have been trained in the traditional model of schooling and have gone through a sort of cognitive boot camp are marveling at the possibility of utilizing generative AI for the more mechanistic tasks, but can do so, almost paradoxically, because they have not had to rely on this very tool to arrive at a position where they can fully exploit it. The big concern is whether the continued use of AI may hinder the capacity to understand its potential uses and also limitations.

- **Accuracy of information and inappropriate content**. As we have seen, because of their very nature and how they are built, even the most advanced generative AI systems are not error proof, and they may generate, albeit if in a very low statistical percentage, content that may be erroneous or inappropriate. Once more, we can already surmise that the continued use of these tools may very well hinder the development of these sort of antibodies to detect such content, as well as that its use should always be supervised by a teacher or adult.

- **The content bubble**. As wide and all-encompassing as the knowledge base may be, until these pre-trained models are superseded by more organic generative AI applications that can up onto the real time Internet, they will be limited to a subset of reality whose limits are unknown. Since this very data set upon which, for example, ChatGPT has been based on, gives the illusion of infinity, it would be very easy for learners to mistake what amounts to a humongous encyclopedia for the real world organic development of

knowledge.
- **The "good enough" effect**. In most cases, ChatGPT and other generative AI applications create content that looks very plausible, and that can even pass judgment for most casual and educated learners. And, even though the results are amazing, and in many cases even experts have been surprised that the generation of ideas and variations that have not occurred to them, the fact remains that it is a sequence of guessing what the next best word would be and not a genuine expression of learning and creativity. This may generate what is known as the "good enough" effect, producing content that is of a very high standard but cannot match the real output of an expert, both in terms of depth and creativity. The big problem with creating content that passes as being top-level is that only the experts can tell the difference, and for most uses what the AI can generate is, as we have stated, good enough, those resulting that only in a potential subtle but real degradation of content, but also in very concrete risks regarding job losses.

Some of the risks involved will, undoubtedly, only be realized as time goes by and generative AI tools are used in earnest in the learning process in schools, but we can already predict that as powerful as ChatGPT and these other applications are, they are also inherently risky, and that is, exactly, the purpose of this text, to remain alert about the risk that focus on the very many positive applications that will transform learning as we know it.

## *All-purpose applications*

Before delving into the intricacies of grade levels, cognitive skills, and specific subject matters, let's first sketch a broad overview of the potential that AI-powered tools hold in revolutionizing the education sector.

The true strength and potential of ChatGPT does not merely lie in listing its diverse applications - a feat we will strive to achieve regardless. More profoundly, it resides in the unique, innovative applications that each educator can best adapt and contextualize to their needs, mirroring the inherent customizability that has always been characteristic of education.

Here are some of the general-purpose applications of ChatGPT and AI powered software:

- **An all-encompassing expert in all areas**. Despite the fact that the knowledge base upon which ChatGPT is based is a closed one, and, as we have said, whatever information is not in the database does not exist for the system, for all intents and purposes, it means that ChatGPT can be equated to an expert in all subject areas. In effect, its continued use demonstrates that it covers a very wide range of subject matters, themes and topics, and it would be highly improbable that any request made even in the most advanced areas within a K-12 curriculum could be excluded from its database. A very notable exception, as of this writing, has to do with its cutoff date of September 2021, but it is expected that the knowledge base will almost certainly be updated beyond that date.
- **A personalized tutor**. Without a doubt, ChatGPT´s superpower, when it comes to education, is the possibility of answering, to an extent, degree, detail, any questions that a learner might have about a particular theme, topic, or even a text input by the user. From a math problem to a poem, ChatGPT will unerringly and patiently answer any and all questions we may have, breaking down even the most complex topics to our needs and understanding. This is a unique and unprecedented feature, which truly can revolutionize education and make true on the long defaulted promise of personalized education.
- **Transcription**. Several applications already exist that offer high fidelity, high accuracy transcriptions of audio or video files, including the most popular streaming services such as

YouTube.
- **Summarization**. Any text that is entered into ChatGPT or some other ad hoc applications can be summarized, main points extracted, ideas identified, and rewritten to address any learning needs.
- **Simplification**. Texts can be rewritten with a lower level of complexity or even adapted specifically to age or grade levels, so as to make them easier to understand.
- **Special needs and learning difficulties**. The system already encodes characteristics of some of the most common learning difficulties, such as dyslexia, and even some other mental health conditions such as various degrees of autism, and can rewrite and adapt texts to better facilitate learning for children with special needs. These very time-consuming jobs, which have become necessary but very tedious tasks to be carried out by learning specialists, can, once more, be personalized to the ultimate level for each student, and accomplished in just a few seconds.
- **Research**. Despite the temporal issue outlined above, the September 2021 current cutoff date, ChatGPT still contains a very comprehensive database that allows for students to use it as a primary source of research, including references and citations to the user's wishes and desires. The advantages over Google or any other search engine are tremendous in the flexibility to perform a la carte, as well as the level of customization, explanation, and how it combines data from various sources in a format that befits exactly what the learner requires.
- **Coding**. Even though our current analysis is more related to general uses for education, as well documented already, ChatGPT is able to generate snippets of code or full-fledged apps and utilities, given the right prompts. Utilizing ChatGPT a programmer requires technical knowledge on the part of the user, but it can be definitely a lifesaver when it comes to generating routines, functions or even many

web-based applications.
- **Images, videos and presentations**. Even though we will analyze, in greater detail, AI related applications to image, video and presentations, especially in terms of what it means for artistic and multimedia expression, there already are numerous applications that can generate unbelievably detailed images, and some applications are now emerging that can create presentations, both in terms of their content as well as their graphic design. Videos are one order of magnitude more difficult, but there are, already, some incipient apps that promise to deliver on text to video generation.
- **Text to speech**. This is not a particularly new application, and one whose use was quite widespread even before AI. However, the current AI voice generation standards are infinitely better than anything we have seen before, and these applications have become even more ubiquitous and easier to use.
- **New content generation**. ChatGPT can already generate customized content, for any subject area and grade level, combining, analyzing, devising lesson plans and personalized learning paths for each student.
- **Conversations**. Right now, students can engage in conversations about any topic, that any grade level, and practice their skills, whether it is for a foreign language that their learning, or even their own native language, within which can be tailored as a nonjudgmental, positive reinforcement environment for students.
- **Impersonating famous characters**. An intriguing and then presented possibility is chatting with a historical figure, famous person or fictional character. ChatGPT can already respond very appropriately to a prompt that initiates a chat sequence with "answer is if you were...", with some amazing results, even when it comes to bridging time and analyzing current events from the perspective of a hero of the past.

## Expected future developments

For the time being, ChatGPT is an entirely textual interface, only being able to communicate with the user via texts. This will probably change very soon, leading to the possibility of entering images, audio and even video as a starting point for a learning activity. There are some concrete references that GPT 4 can already generate cognitive results from just a photograph or image, and produce content as needed.

When we come to think of it, this is not surprising since image recognition was always at the heart of deep learning and neural networks, so being able to receive input in the form of images is only a natural step in its development. It is very probable that the bandwidth needed for image input as compared to text, may be the principal reason why this is not a feature available, at this time, to the general public.

## Reading

Both ChatGPT as well as an ever-growing variety of applications can perform a number of tasks associated with reading, which, as we know, and rightly so, is one of the main skills that are to be acquired by students at school. Reading legitimately sits atop the hierarchy of cognitive skills, so much so that it is often universally considered the main indicator for progress in learning, as in "reading above or below grade level".

Generative AI applications are formidable tools that can greatly enhance reading, especially in the ability to endlessly customize text processing, which constitutes the superpower of ChatGPT and these other applications.

Here are some possible applications to reading.
- **Summarizing**, analyzing main points in a text. The system can perform, to an infinite level of customization, any activities associated with reading comprehension, whether

summarization, extracting main points of ideas explaining key points, simplifying the text, or making any necessary adaptations for students with dyslexia or other learning issues.

- **Reading comprehension assistance**: ChatGPT can be utilized to help students with reading comprehension by answering questions about the text, explaining difficult concepts or vocabulary. In this context, a key feature of ChatGPT is that it concatenates messages referring to an initial text and does not need to be reminded of his existence, allowing students to potentially answer successive questions without having to reenter the original text.
- **Rewrite a text** for any age or grade level, simplifying it as needed.
- In bullet points, or in any other format, **extract the main ideas or concepts**.
- **Perform sentiment analysis**, detecting the overall tone of the text.
- **Personalized reading plans**. AI can create personalized reading plans for students based on their reading levels, interests, and progress, adapting the content to suit their needs and ensure they remain engaged and that their learning curve is optimal.
- Identify **entities and references** in a given text.
- Rewrite to better suit students with **special learning needs**.
- **Rewrite to change the tone** to a more positive one, eliminate threatening words, customize for students with emotional issues.
- Rewrite a text in the **style of any writer**.
- **Text-to-speech conversion**: AI applications can convert written content to audio, supporting students with learning disabilities or those who are auditory learners.
- **Change formats**, that is, reprocess texts into any literary form.

- **Rewrite with alternative endings**, or changes in the narrative or plot.
- **Analyze any text** for biases, hidden meanings, or anything else associated with better comprehension of the text.

Anticipating what is a deeper philosophical discussion, which we will deal with later in the text, it is almost self-evident that reading comprehension and a set of skills associated with decoding, analyzing, extracting main points and ideas, are cognitive skills that are at risk of becoming obsolete or redundant, since AI powered systems can do them with ultimate efficiency and greater speed. In theory, there is no more need for anybody to read a long book, or to painstakingly process a complex text, abilities that were considered paramount and the ultimate embodiment of academic success.

The value of developing reading comprehension skills transcends its mere utility to process vast amounts of text as a way to learn, but it can also be argued that, by virtue of the existence of these systems, anybody can read a lot more in a lot less time, thus possibly learning more. Again, later in the text we will get deeper into this, and reflect on the evolution of certain cognitive skills and the risks associated with their potential loss, but we immediately need to be aware of a seemingly irreconcilable tension between how we learn, the skills associated with the learning process, and the perennial quest for learning that lies at the heart of education.

## *Writing*

Producing comprehensive, well-thought-out, properly developed writing is at the heart of what we considered to be essential developmental skills in students, and the venerable 4000 word essay or research paper still constitutes, to this day, the ultimate embodiment of academic prowess.

It is beyond the scope and purpose of the current text to try to analyze the reasons why writing attained such a preeminence in school curricula worldwide, but the benefits of writing comprise being able to express one's own ideas, in a medium that, if anything, became even more ubiquitous on the age of the Internet, with the potential for unlimited personal expression in a horizontalized, democratized learning landscape.

Generative AI provides users with amazing and unlimited capabilities for generating written content. Literally, and it also n, anything can be produced by ChatGPT and many other ad hoc applications.

These are some of the mind-boggling applications of AI to writing:

- **Generating outlines** for any given topic or idea.
- **Writing any form of text in any style** and to any word length, including essays, research papers, scientific writing, fiction, nonfiction, a truly unlimited infinite treasure trove of writing styles and possibilities.
- **Rewrite text to improve it** or to change it to a certain style.
- Include **references and citations** to any given standard.
- Perform research on the fly and produce text based on that research, including numerical data and URLs.
- **Improve, correct, rewrite, edit** and provide suggestions for any text that is input into the system, customizing the output to whatever level is desired.
- **Check for accuracy, fact check**, detect any possible errors in content.

When it comes to how to use AI applications for writing in the context of schools, and the learning process for students to become writers, once more, we will not engage, for the time being, in the philosophical discussion of how much is it that students will need to learn in the current and future context when it comes to producing their original pieces of writing, i.e., is it acceptable that the de facto motor writing for any person in the future will not be to start from a blank page?

In that context, the suggestions that ensue are based on

the current model of learning how to write, meaning that the objective, for schools overall, is to progress in the ability to produce increasingly complex piece of writing and to allow students to be able to generate fully fledged autonomous writing when they graduate from high school.

- **Grammar and style correction**: AI can automatically detect and correct grammar, spelling, and punctuation errors, as well as suggest improvements in writing style, tone, and clarity.
- **Personalized feedback**: AI can provide real-time, personalized feedback on writing, helping writers improve their skills and develop a more refined writing style.
- **Writer's assistance**: AI-powered chatbots, like ChatGPT, can offer support during the writing process, answering questions, providing suggestions, and helping with research.
- **Writing templates**: AI can generate customizable writing templates, providing structure and guidance for various types of documents, from essays to business proposals.
- **Act as an editor** for whatever purposes are required, suggesting modifications to the students written text, to better suit what is required.
- **Thesaurus**, personalized suggestions. When in the process of writing, AI can produce on the spot customized recommendations such as words, appropriate metaphors, synonyms, ideas to complete a certain paragraph or plot.
- When developing outlines, before a student sets out to write, AI can **suggest improvements** and even point out themes, topics and ideas that may not have been included in the original outline.
- **Collaborative writing**. AI can be an excellent assistant and collaborator for writing, even alternating the writing of sentences and paragraphs, helping students who may otherwise have difficulties in going through a complete assignment.

Some specific ideas for different grade levels include:

Elementary School:

- Story prompts: Use of AI-generated prompts to inspire students to create short stories or paragraphs, helping them develop creativity and writing fluency.
- Vocabulary building: AI can provide context-appropriate vocabulary suggestions to encourage students to expand their word usage and improve their writing.
- Writing buddies: ChatcGPT can serve as a supportive writing buddy, offering encouragement and answering questions as students practice their writing skills.

Middle School:

- Peer collaboration: AI can facilitate collaborative writing projects by connecting students, providing prompts, and helping them give and receive feedback.
- Interactive storytelling: Students can engage in AI-powered interactive stories that adapt based on their choices, promoting creative thinking and narrative development.
- Essay organization: AI can help students outline and organize their essays, providing guidance on structure, thesis statements, and topic sentences.

High School:

- Research assistance: AI-powered chatbots can help students find and evaluate sources, making research tasks more efficient and effective.
- Personalized feedback: AI can provide detailed, real-time feedback on student writing, targeting areas for improvement and suggesting resources for further learning.
- Revision and editing: AI can aid students in the revision and editing process, pointing out errors, inconsistencies, and areas that need improvement,

while also suggesting alternative phrasing or style adjustments.

## Learning foreign languages

Another of the mainstream applications of ChatGPT and other generative AI applications is, as expected, the learning of foreign languages. Its uncanny ability to provide almost endless customization comes in very handily when confronted with the usually difficult task of mastering a new language and finding a counterpart who can match and accompany our progressive acquisition of the language.

Some of the possible applications to the learning of foreign languages include:

- **Correcting**, making suggestions and generally helping foreign-language students to improve their language skills in any form desired.
- **Conversation**. ChatGPT, as of this writing, can easily be customized to any level in the language, so that it provides a much-needed conversation partner at whatever level the student requires. At the same time, it can correct any errors and make suggestions for improved language skills.
- **Personalized texts**. As with regular reading applications, when it comes to learning a foreign language, ChatGPT can provide a customized text on any topic that were interested in ,and to the level that the student requires, so that it can be comprehended with the adequate level of difficulty. It can even suggest a progression of increasingly more challenging texts so as to improve in the desired proficiency.
- **Vocabulary**, synonyms, rewriting in simpler form. Any word or expression that is unclear, synonyms, or even rewriting a text to make it less complex is within the available range of possibilities in ChatGPT. Although this was available in other online applications such as Google

translator, the ease of use, speed and accuracy of ChatGPT are, as of yet, unmatched.

- **Translation of any text** that might be of interest. Many of us who have struggled to learn a foreign language have been stuck with endless textual renderings of inconsequential tales and stories that we were totally uninterested in, but these large language models can make learning fun by translating, and even to any level that we require, any text of any topic that we could be interested in, thus personalizing the context to our ultimate whims and desires.

A particularly attractive application is the extrapolation of text to speech capabilities, natural language processing and speech recognition, all of which are now readily available separately, to provide users with a seamless oral conversation engine that allows them to practice not just textual but a real conversation, once more, tailored to the level of proficiency desired.

And we are not far from real-time translation, whereby headphones connected to speech recognition can the code spoken language, translated into the desired other language and reproduce it in the person's ear as if they were listening to their native language. This will undoubtedly become a mainstream application in the very near future and may even render the learning of foreign languages almost obsolete.

## Summary

*Risks Associated with AI in Education:*

- Inhibiting cognitive skills
- Dependence on AI
- Accuracy of information and inappropriate content

- Content limitations and the "good enough" effect

*General-Purpose Applications of AI in Education:*

- Acting as an expert in all subject areas
- Providing personalized tutoring
- Transcription of audio and video files
- Summarization of text
- Simplification of complex texts
- Catering to special needs and learning difficulties
- Assisting with research
- Supporting coding activities
- Generating images, videos, and presentations
- Enabling text-to-speech capabilities
- Creating new content and lesson plans
- Facilitating conversations and language practice
- Allowing interactions with historical or fictional characters

Expected Future Developments:
- AI systems evolving to accept image, audio, and video inputs
- Potential for generating content based on visual prompts

Applications of AI in Reading:
- Summarizing and analyzing main points in a text
- Assisting with reading comprehension by answering questions and explaining difficult concepts
- Rewriting texts for different age or grade levels
- Extracting main ideas or concepts in bullet points or other formats
- Performing sentiment analysis to detect the overall tone of a text
- Creating personalized reading plans based on students'

levels, interests, and progress
- Identifying entities and references in a text
- Adapting texts for students with special learning needs or emotional issues
- Rewriting texts in the style of different writers
- Converting text to speech for auditory learners
- Changing formats of texts into different literary forms
- Rewriting texts with alternative endings or changes in the narrative or plot
- Analyzing texts for biases and hidden meanings

*Applications of AI in Writing:*

- Generating outlines for different topics or ideas
- Writing texts in various styles and word lengths, including essays, research papers, fiction, and nonfiction
- Rewriting texts to improve or change their style
- Including references and citations according to specific standards
- Performing research and producing text based on that research
- Improving, correcting, and suggesting changes to written text
- Providing grammar and style correction, including spelling and punctuation
- Offering personalized feedback on writing
- Assisting writers during the writing process, answering questions and providing suggestions
- Creating writing templates for different types of documents
- Serving as an editor, suggesting modifications to written text
- Providing thesaurus and personalized word suggestions
- Assisting with outlining and organizing essays
- Facilitating collaborative writing projects

- Supporting peer collaboration and feedback

*Applications of AI in Learning Foreign Languages:*

- Correcting, making suggestions, and helping improve language skills
- Engaging in conversation practice with customized language proficiency levels
- Providing personalized texts for language learning with appropriate difficulty levels
- Offering vocabulary assistance, synonyms, and text simplification
- Translating texts of interest into the target language
- Enabling real-time translation and speech recognition for seamless oral conversation practice
- Anticipating future developments in real-time translation and potentially rendering the learning of foreign languages obsolete.

## *Prompts and activities*

**General-purpose applications**
- Ask ChatGPT anything about any topic, in the natural language, as if you were asking an all-knowing teacher.
- ChatGPT can refer to a topic that it finds in its database as well as any text entered by the user, and, as of this writing, even read PDFs through external plug-ins.
- Explain …. in greater detail.
- Give an example to illustrate the point.

- Ask any question, again, as you would ask a person. For example, if somebody is trying to learn about the second world war, ChatGPT can answer questions like "what would have happened if Churchill had not been named Prime Minister at the onset of the war?"
- Explain again in simpler terms.
- ChatGPT is also surprisingly adept at understanding colloquial language. For example," I need to understand.... better"
- Answer the question so that a .... grader or ...-year-old child would understand it.
- Give your answer so that it can be easily read and understood by a dyslexic person.
- Provide an answer that can be read by a person in the autistic spectrum.
- Direct research questions can be asked, such as, for example, "write a 1000 word essay on evidence for life on Mars".
- Research can be customized to the user's needs, including, for example, "include all references and citations in APA style, as well as URLs of sites used in the investigation" NOTE: it must be stated that here is where even GPT 4 still incurs in hallucinations, not infrequently quoting papers that do not exist or are very hard to find and corroborate (any coincidences with real life...)
- Write xxxx (programming language) code to ... (Describe what is required here)
- Write a fictional account of how, in the future, the United States becomes a country that uses only renewable energies and has a zero carbon footprint: NOTE: there are safeguards in ChatGPT and many of

the other generative AI systems to prevent from even developing pretended scenarios that are negative in any way, including war, violence, or any negative consequences.

- Write a story about.... Include the following... And one of the protagonists is...
- Compare and contrast the education systems of...
- Answer is if you were ... Any subsequent questions in that chat would be answered not as the ChatGPT AI but rather the person or even fictional character that has been specified. This is a fantastic opportunity for interactive and engaging learning for students, especially the younger ones.
- Simulated scenarios. For example, I am Franklin Roosevelt and I want to replicate the negotiations that took place in Yalta conference. For the following questions and dialogue, please answer as either Joseph Stalin or Winston Churchill.
- Create a dialogue between, for example, Albert Einstein and Marie Curie on what it means to be a pioneer scientist and the difficulties they face in their respective careers.
- I want to role-play being a journalist, so pretend that you are.... and answer my questions as you would if you were at a media interview.

**Reading**

- Summarize the following text (or PDF at a certain URL) in XXXX words.

NOTE: ChatGPT also knows about hundreds of thousands of books, so, in all likelihood, it will also be able to perform the same functions on books that it has "read" during its training.

- Find the main ideas and write them in bullet points.
- Simplify the text so that it can be understood by a xxx -year-old.
- Simplify the text so that it can be more easily read by a student with dyslexia.
- I don't understand the paragraph that starts with… Please explain it to me.
- What does it mean when they say "…"?
- Any conventional reading comprehension question, such as, what did the author intend to convey as the main theme for the book, importance and significance of characters and events.
- Detect any hidden biases in the following text.
- Validate the following text and fact check it for any errors or inaccuracies.
- Analyze the general emotional tone and sentiment of the text, providing examples of what you base yourself on, and rewrite it in a more optimistic tone.
- Rewrites this text so that it ends with… Or suggest a three alternative endings.
- Rewrite it into a boy, or sonnet, or a theater play.
- Identify entities, URLs, references, any learning materials are mentioned in the text.

## Writing

- Write (Style) (Length) (Topic) (Number of words)
- Write an outline for…
- Include chapters and items for each chapter
- Write a story involving (characters) with the following story line…
- Rewrite with an alternative ending…

- Check the following text for grammar and punctuation.
- Suggest improvements to the following text.
- Write an introduction for...
- Write the next (...) paragraphs for the following text.
- Complete the following phrase.
- Rewrite this text as a (play – dialogue – poem – essay)
- Check the following text for facts, detect any possible content errors.
- Give me feedback on this text, improve my writing style, make it more (formal – conversational – scientific)
- Suggest synonyms for the following word – phrases.
- Suggest other themes and ideas for the following outline:

**Foreign Languages**
- Translate...
- I am a (beginner – intermediate – advanced) student of ..., chat with me at my level.
- Create a text at ... level on .... (topic)
- Translate the following URL to ... level.
- Correct this text and make suggestions.

## Sample Activity

<u>Lesson Plan</u>: Being an Influencer During the French Revolution

**Overview**

In this cross-disciplinary project, students will research the

French Revolution and apply their understanding to create an Instagram profile for a fictional character living through the era. Students will write posts that demonstrate their understanding of the causes, events, and impacts of the French Revolution.

## Objectives

By the end of this unit, students will be able to:

1. Describe the key events and causes of the French Revolution.
2. Create a timeline of major events during the French Revolution.
3. Apply their understanding of the French Revolution to a creative, modern context.
4. Effectively use digital resources, including ChatGPT, to gather and summarize information.

## Resources

1. Access to ChatGPT
2. Internet for research
3. Instagram template for profile creation

Duration: 5 Sessions

Session 1: Introduction and Research

Objective

Students will begin their research on the French Revolution using ChatGPT and other internet resources. By the end of the session, they should have a basic understanding of the French Revolution and the events and ideas that shaped it.

## Duration

One class session (45-60 minutes)

Materials Needed

- Computers or tablets with internet access

## Activity

1. Introduction : Begin the session by introducing the French Revolution to the students. Briefly explain the significance of the event and how it reshaped French society and influenced the world.

2. ChatGPT Exploration (25 minutes): Introduce students to ChatGPT. Explain what ChatGPT is, how it works, and how it can be used as a research tool.

Here is a brief guide on how to use ChatGPT for this research:

- Ask specific questions: For example, "What were the causes of the French Revolution?" or "Who were the key figures in the French Revolution?"
- Ask for summaries: For instance, "Can you summarize the events of the French Revolution?" or "Can you summarize the impact of the French Revolution on French society?"
- Use prompts for creative thinking: Such as, "Imagine you are a common citizen during the French Revolution. What might you experience?"

Encourage students to take notes from the responses they receive from ChatGPT.

3. Independent Research (15 minutes): After students have interacted with ChatGPT, allow them to explore more about the French Revolution on the internet. They can visit reputable history websites or digital libraries to expand their knowledge.

## Homework

Ask students to continue their individual research on the French Revolution at home. They should focus on understanding the causes, key events, impacts, and the daily life of people during that time. Remind them that they can use

ChatGPT as well as the internet for this research. They should watch the following video:

Title: "The French Revolution: Crash Course World History 29"

Link: Crash Course World History: French Revolution https://www.youtube.com/watch?v=lTTvKwCylFY

Summary: This video provides a brief but comprehensive overview of the French Revolution, explaining its causes, key events, and impacts. The host presents the information in an engaging, accessible way that is perfect for high school students.

Students can use Generative AI plugins to obtain the transcript and summarize the main points using ChatGPT

Session 2: Digital Timeline Creation

**Objective**

By the end of this session, students should be able to create a detailed and accurate digital timeline of the key events during the French Revolution.

**Duration**

One class session (45-60 minutes)

**Materials Needed**

- Research notes from Session 1
- Computers or tablets with internet access

**Activity**

1. Group Discussion: Divide the students into small groups. Ask them to share their research findings from Session 1 with each other. Discuss the major events and figures they discovered, the causes and impacts of the French Revolution, and the life of common people during this period.

2. Timeline Tools Introduction (10 minutes): Introduce students to digital tools they can use to create their timelines. Suggested tools include:

[Tiki-Toki](https://www.tiki-toki.com/): A web-based software for creating beautiful interactive timelines that can be shared on the internet.

[TimeGraphics](https://time.graphics/: A flexible tool for creating, collaborating on, and sharing timelines.

[Sutori](https://www.sutori.com/): A collaborative instruction and presentation tool for the classroom.

Give a brief demonstration of how to use the chosen tool and explain the criteria for the timeline (e.g., it should include key events, dates, brief descriptions, and visuals representing each event).

3. Digital Timeline Creation with ChatGPT: Students will start creating their digital timelines in their groups. They can use ChatGPT to verify dates, ask for more details about specific events, or to understand the sequence of events. For example, students can ask ChatGPT questions like, "What are the key events of the French Revolution in chronological order?" or "What happened during the Reign of Terror?"

To ensure accuracy and depth of information, students should cross-check the information they get from ChatGPT with other reliable resources. Encourage them to make their timelines detailed and visually engaging.

Homework

Students continue refining the digital timeline and start thinking about the fictional character they will create. They should consider the events on their timeline and think about how a common person living through the French Revolution might have experienced those events.

## Assessment

Evaluate students' digital timelines for accuracy, clarity, detail, and creativity. Check to see if they have included all the major events of the French Revolution in the correct chronological order. This can be a formative assessment to guide further instruction and group discussions.

### Session 3: Instagram Profile Creation

**Objective**

By the end of this session, students should be able to create a detailed Instagram profile for a fictional character living during the French Revolution.

**Duration**

One class session (45-60 minutes)

**Materials Needed**

- Research notes and timelines from previous sessions
- Computers or tablets with internet access
- Instagram profile template

**Activity**

1. Instagram Profile Introduction : Begin by explaining what an Instagram profile typically includes (username, bio, profile picture, and posts) and show students a few examples of effective Instagram profiles. Discuss what makes these profiles effective (clear descriptions, engaging posts, consistent themes).

2. Character Brainstorming: Ask students to start brainstorming about their fictional character. Who are they? What is their social status? How are they involved in the French Revolution? Encourage them to think about how their character might react to the events they have included on their timeline.

3. Instagram Profile Creation: Students start creating their Instagram profile using the template. They should come up with an appropriate username and bio that reflects their character's personality and circumstances during the French Revolution. They should also consider what kind of profile picture their character might have.

4. ChatGPT Consultation: After creating their initial profile, students can use ChatGPT to verify if their character and profile align with the era of the French Revolution. They could ask ChatGPT questions like, "Does this profile accurately reflect a person living during the French Revolution?" or "Could a common citizen during the French Revolution have these views?" ChatGPT can provide feedback based on its extensive knowledge base.

**Homework**

Students continue developing the Instagram profile at home. They should start thinking about the types of posts their character would create during the major events of the French Revolution.

**Assessment**

Evaluate students' Instagram profiles for historical accuracy, creativity, and detail. Check to see if the character they have created would make sense in the context of the French Revolution. This can be a formative assessment to help guide the next steps of the project.

Session 4: Writing Instagram Posts

**Objective**

By the end of this session, students should have written at

least five Instagram posts for their character that reflect key events of the French Revolution.

## Duration

One class session (45-60 minutes)

## Materials Needed

- Instagram profiles from Session 3
- Research notes and timelines from previous sessions
- Computers or tablets with internet access

## Activity

1. Writing Posts : Students begin by writing at least five Instagram posts from the perspective of their character. These posts should reflect the key events on their timeline and demonstrate an understanding of the French Revolution. They can include images, hashtags, and captions as if their character were witnessing and responding to the events of the Revolution.

2. ChatGPT Verification : After writing their posts, students can consult ChatGPT to check their posts for historical accuracy. They can ask, "Would this be an accurate post for a common citizen to make during the Reign of Terror?" or "Does this post accurately reflect the events of the French Revolution?"

3. Group Interaction : After verifying their posts for accuracy, students should share their profiles and posts with other groups. Each group will like and comment on other groups' posts, simulating an actual Instagram interaction. They can ask questions, add reactions, or even comment as if they were another character from the same time period.

## Homework

Students finalize their Instagram posts and prepare for their final presentations. They should also think about how they will explain their character's reactions to the events of the French Revolution.

**Assessment**

Assess the Instagram posts for historical accuracy, creativity, and depth of understanding of the French Revolution. Assess the interaction between groups for relevance, thoughtfulness, and adherence to the character's perspective. This can be a formative assessment to help guide the final presentation.

### Session 5: Final Presentation and Gallery Walk

**Objective**

By the end of this session, students should be able to present their Instagram profiles to the class, explaining their character's experiences during the French Revolution. They should also be able to engage with other students' presentations and provide thoughtful feedback.

**Duration**

One class session (45-60 minutes)

**Materials Needed**

- Completed Instagram profiles and posts
- Poster boards for displaying the Instagram profiles
- Computers or tablets with internet access

Activity

1. Final Preparations: Students prepare for their presentations by finalizing their Instagram profiles and posts. They print out or display their profiles and posts on poster boards.

2. Gallery Setup: Arrange the classroom for a gallery walk. Each group should set up their poster board in a

designated space around the room.

3. Open Class Invitation: Send out invitations to families, school administrators, and other classes to attend the open class. This will provide an authentic audience for students' work and encourage them to present their best effort.

4. Gallery Walk and Presentations: Students, along with visiting families and other attendees, walk around the gallery, reading the Instagram posts and learning about each character's perspective on the French Revolution. Each group will stand by their poster board to explain their character and answer any questions.

5. Group Feedback : After all groups have presented, facilitate a group discussion. Ask students what they learned from the project, what they found most interesting about other groups' Instagram profiles, and how this activity changed their understanding of the French Revolution.

**Assessment**

Assess the final Instagram profiles and posts for historical accuracy, creativity, and depth of understanding of the French Revolution. Also, evaluate the group presentations for clarity, coherence, and the ability to answer questions about their character. The feedback from the group discussion can also provide insight into each group's engagement with the project. This will be a summative assessment.

**Note**

Ensure to inform the students, families, and all attendees that the Instagram profiles and posts are fictitious and meant for educational purposes. This will help avoid any misunderstandings about the nature of the project.

## Assessment Rubric for Instagram Profile Project

Research & Understanding of the French Revolution

- Excellent: Demonstrates a deep understanding of the French Revolution. Research is thorough and all findings are accurately represented.
- Good: Demonstrates a clear understanding of the French Revolution. Research is largely complete and most findings are accurately represented.
- Satisfactory: Demonstrates a basic understanding of the French Revolution. Research is somewhat complete and some findings are accurately represented.
- Needs Improvement: Demonstrates little understanding of the French Revolution. Research is incomplete and few findings are accurately represented.

Instagram Profile

- Excellent: Profile effectively and creatively represents a fictional character living during the French Revolution. The username, bio, and profile picture are appropriate and engaging.
- Good: Profile represents a fictional character living during the French Revolution. The username, bio, and profile picture are mostly appropriate.
- Satisfactory: Profile somewhat represents a fictional character living during the French Revolution. The username, bio, or profile picture could use improvement.
- Needs Improvement: Profile does not adequately represent a fictional character living during the French Revolution. The username, bio, and profile picture are inappropriate or off-topic.

Instagram Posts

- Excellent: Posts accurately reflect the events of the French Revolution and demonstrate a deep understanding of their impact. They are creative and engaging, effectively representing the character's

perspective.
- Good: Posts mostly reflect the events of the French Revolution and demonstrate a good understanding of their impact. They mostly represent the character's perspective.
- Satisfactory: Posts somewhat reflect the events of the French Revolution and demonstrate a basic understanding of their impact. They somewhat represent the character's perspective.
- Needs Improvement: Posts do not adequately reflect the events of the French Revolution or demonstrate an understanding of their impact. They do not effectively represent the character's perspective.

Presentation & Gallery Walk
- Excellent: The group presents their project effectively, demonstrating a deep understanding of their character and the French Revolution. They answer all questions clearly and confidently.
- Good: The group presents their project well, demonstrating a good understanding of their character and the French Revolution. They answer most questions clearly.
- Satisfactory: The group presents their project, demonstrating a basic understanding of their character and the French Revolution. They answer some questions clearly.
- Needs Improvement: The group struggles to present their project and demonstrate an understanding of their character and the French Revolution. They struggle to answer questions clearly.

# OTHER APPLICATIONS

We will now analyze some of the other more specific applications to learning that can target subjects other than reading, writing and foreign languages. This is not, by any means, a taxonomy, since, literally, effective uses for learning are infinite, and it may very well be one of the distinguishing traits of future great teachers that they are able to exploit ChatGPT and other similar apps to the full extent of their potential in ways that are creative and imaginative.

## *Math and Science*

Perennially considered some of the toughest subjects to master in the school context, Science and Mathematics are also wonderful playing fields for generative AI applications. Here are some of them:

- **Solving numeric problems**. Current capabilities of ChatGPT are truly amazing when it comes to solving numeric problems, both mathematical as well as applications to any science. The system can provide very detailed explanations, break down topics to the level of simplicity required, and provide greater detail and even alternative methods for any step in them.
- **Applications to more complex mathematical interfaces**. The very popular Wolphram Alpha, one of the most widely used mathematical applications, has already developed a ChatGPT plug-in, and Khan Academy is also incorporating

its own version of ChatGPT for its knowledge interface, just to cite two examples that have been pioneers in the incorporation of the ChatGPT API to their systems. This would allow for more intuitive use of any of these powerful applications, and extend current ChatGPT capabilities to the interpretation and production of, for example, graphs and other more complex mathematical solutions.

- **Solving any type of word problems**. The same applies to any word problem for Science or Math, in terms of being able to solve it, respond to any level of detail required, and provide explanations and answers to any depth or complexity.
- **Creating practice problems.** After solving one or several problems, we can ask ChatGPT to create any number of similar problems for us to practice, together with their explained answers that we can occur to if needed. Even for the more conventional type of assessment, this is a godsend, since procuring similar test questions to anything that we were going to sit for has always been at a premium in terms of preparing for examinations.
- **Simulations**. There are many things that schools cannot do, from dangerous experiments to those a record of very expensive equipment, and these generative AI systems can simulate experiments, together with their results, as well as laboratory templates or sample reports so that students can calculate results and formulate conclusions.
- **Creating engaging problems and activities** for students to solve. Any math or science educator can relate to how hard it is to come up with a well-rounded problem that starts from a real-life situation or case study, for example, in forensics or space exploration, which can have students integrate math and science whilst becoming excited about a real life challenge. This is completely within the realm of what these applications can do: a prompt that specifies the concepts we wish to include, level of difficulty, the type of case that we want, and ChatGPT will come up

with any number of ideas for engaging, thought-provoking problems for students to reach out beyond their regular more abstract exercises that they engage in.
- **Real-life connections**. For any science or math related discipline, it is just enough to ask ChatGPT to provide some examples of real life applications of any science or math concept, for it to come up with answers to students eternal battle cry when presented with a topic "what is this useful for?".
- **Erroneous data, paradoxes, or perplexing situations**. It is a preferred critical thinking resource for science and math teachers to devise problems that contain some kind of data that throws either an impossible result, a paradoxical one, or anything that can make students think about more than the mechanics of solving the problem, and to help them acquire the much-needed scale of having an intuitive appreciation for biased or erroneous data. Once more, a prompt that asks ChatGPT to simulate a data set that includes an out of range are impossible result will yield the desired data.
- **Data analysis**. Feeding results of any real-life process or measurement, even automatically through sensors, can help students analyze data and provide any kind of statistical measures that can be useful for the learning process. This can help students go directly to the data analysis piece, to interpret results and make inferences and conclusions.

Once more, projected future developments include the ability to input images, not just text, in which case graphs, photographs, or any other non-textual data can be the starting point for any learning activity in the area. Real-time monitoring through sensors that can interface with ChatGPT is also a very promising field supposed to also provide on-the-fly data analysis as required. Generative

## Simulated interactive situations

One of the most fascinating possibilities of ChatGPT and the generative AI family of applications is the reenactment of hypothetical situations and simulated interactive dialogues.

In effect, ChatGPT can easily impersonate any historical or current figure and engage in a conversation as if it were that person, alive or dead. This allows for students to interview any historical figure or current person, asking them any questions they want, and even applying, to the present and/or future, some of the lessons of the past.

In terms of engaging possibilities, one that is particularly fascinating is the creation of fictional dialogues between non-contemporary figures of the past, such as, for example, Socrates and Einstein, or any other gathering of notable figures from the past who may have a lot to say to each other and can provide an invaluable lesson in historical perspective. In that same vibe, another fun activity is to bring back to life some of the heroes from the past and asked them to analyze either the current rise in AI as well as some of the things that are now happening in the world.

Taking this capability one step further, a historical situation may be reenacted with the students as one of its protagonists. I recently tried out asking ChatGPT to reenact the Yalta conference in the second world war, telling the system that I would be Franklin Roosevelt and to answer, alternatively, as either Joseph Stalin or Winston Churchill. The results were utterly fascinating, allowing me to role-play and try to find alternative outcomes and possibilities for that pivotal event in history.

## Social emotional learning

When it comes to social emotional learning, inasmuch as

there are endless fascinating possibilities, we must first consider one of the issues that we mentioned at the beginning, and that is, that despite their unbelievable accuracy and almost infinite knowledge base, because the very nature of the neural networks and deep learning, these models are opaque and never 100% error proof.

When dealing with other subjects, these hallucinations can be detrimental to the learning process, but, in most cases, only become misleading or confusing for student learning. However, when it comes to issues related to social emotional learning, there needs to be adult supervision and some mechanism whereby any such mistakes do not produce undesired consequences within themes and topics that can impact healthy development by students.

Having said this, and allowing for adequate supervision and overseeing the interactions, the possibilities for social emotional learning are endless and unprecedented in terms of levels of engagement and interactivity.

Some of them include:

- **Crafting of stories** with any storyline, moral lessons or situations as befits the curriculum. Generative AI applications can be a dream come true in terms of being able to produce any story, any moral lesson, any and every situation that the teacher would want to use as a catalyst for reflections and/or the learning of values and moral principles. Needless to say, these can be tailored to any age and level of complexity.
- **Role-playing and interactive dialogue**. Any situation can be simulated and ChatGPT can play any part in first person, for students or the teacher to exemplify actions and interventions to mitigate or solve certain problems. Once more, this should be used with caution, and with the teacher present so that, if anything untoward is produced, they are able to handle the situation appropriately and

derive positive lessons from it.
- **Emotional support, advice.** With extreme caution, the system can act as a supportive peer/friend/counselor, since the model, at least for ChatGPT and the date of this writing, is inherently positive and de-biased to eliminate stereotypes and include positive values.
- **Case studies.** Similarly, ChatGPT can generate hypothetical scenarios and case studies for students to suggest alternative resolutions, and even provide them with feedback on some of these possible outcomes that they generate.
- **Emotion Recognition and Response**: Some advanced chatbots are capable of recognizing emotional cues in written language and responding accordingly. This could help learners understand different emotional states and appropriate responses. A particularly interesting example would be to ask ChatGPT to generate a text that is written by a child or a person with certain emotional issues, and for the students to read through it and try to discern what is going on with the person, a kind of diagnostic, fostering empathy and other related values.
- **Mindfulness and Stress Management Techniques**: Chatbots can guide learners through mindfulness exercises or provide tips for managing stress and anxiety.
- **Teaching Digital Citizenship**: Chatbots can help students understand the importance of responsible online behavior, digital etiquette, and the potential consequences of digital footprints, which are essential aspects of being a digital citizen.
- **Conflict Resolution Practice**: Chatbots can simulate scenarios that require conflict resolution, allowing students to practice problem-solving and negotiation skills.

Social emotional learning is, perhaps, one of the fields that holds the most promise when it comes to using the inbred flexibility and infinite customization of ChatGPT to deliver a one-of-a-kind learning experience. Even though it requires very careful monitoring and supervision, the possibilities are endless and, if adequately set up, generative AI can provide a very safe space, for, paradoxically, this most human aspect of education.

## Sports and nutrition

Even though it may seem that these are two areas that are quite far off the reality of artificial intelligence, the personalization feature can come in very handy when it comes to giving each student what they need in terms of their health, physical activity and nutrition.

Some of the possible applications include:

- **Personalized fitness and training plans**. AI can constitute an omniscient personal trainer, who can develop a personalized exercise and fitness plan receiving as inputs anthropometric values for the person in question, as well as their expected diet, body type, etc. These exercise routines can be completely customized to performance in a given sport, losing weight, or any other related objective that the student in question should pursue.
- **Data sheets and other instruments for tracking**. Following up on the previous idea, AI can also generate a spreadsheet type application that can the person monitor their progress, record their activity, and help them, in general, keep track of both exercise and eventually food intake or diet.
- **Nutrition plans and special diets**. A uniquely powerful combination, or even a standalone application is to devise a personalized dietary plan, complete with recipes, purchasing lists for the ingredients, which, once more, can be ultimately customized in terms of calories, dietary requirements, foods that have to be kept off because of allergies or intolerance, and even within a certain budget

- **Injury Prevention and Rehabilitation.** Chatbots can provide information about injury prevention, proper form, and techniques. They can also provide guidance on rehabilitation exercises (although any serious injury should always be addressed by a medical professional).

It is to be expected that, very soon, generative AI will be integrated with wearable devices, such as watches and other devices that track physical activity, so that the record-keeping, analysis, and recommendations can be derived from organic real-life data.

## Other generic applications

The possible uses of ChatGPT and the related family of generative AI applications are literally endless, and it would be clearly the main skill for the next generation of teachers to fully utilize the immense power of these systems for a renewed and more engaging learning experience for students of all ages. The following suggestions are of a general-purpose nature, and can be applied to several subjects:

- **Role-playing scenarios.** Generative AI applications can generate all kinds of role-playing scenarios, from a negotiation, conflict resolution, mystery to be solved, escape rooms, almost anything that the imagination can conjure come be simulated by these systems, albeit if with successive prompts on the part of the teacher until the desired scenario is achieved. Needless to say, these role-playing simulations, which, once more, come be customized to any subject matter and grade level, are infinitely more engaging, hands-on, and constitute authentic and relevant learning experiences for students.
- **Case studies.** Similarly, case studies can be generated to exemplify any type of situation, complete with answer key, reflections, possible different outcomes, and even

suggested Q&A's for discussion and debates.
- **Virtual travel**. All kinds of virtual travel scenarios can also be created by generative AI applications. Planning a trip, creating mystery clues about a place that needs to be guessed, international food, responding as a local of any place in location, generating vernacular cultural expressions, these systems can provide their users with the ultimate virtual travel experience, which, once again, can bring life to any geography of social studies classroom in ways that are unique and unprecedented.
- **Time travel**. Similarly, in any context for any subject, teachers can instruct ChatGPT to transport users to not just another place but also another time, providing the now usual level of interactivity and customization but going back in time or, maybe, even to a projected future. In effect, a prompt can be generated to instruct the system to provide contextual answers for a simulated future scenario, described in detail in the prompt itself.
- **Test preparation**. ChatGPT can act as a virtual instructor, testing students' knowledge and providing them with questions, giving them feedback, helping them revise or prepare even for conventional assessments like exams.
- **Interpreting rules and regulations**. ChatGPT has already amassed a vast knowledge about local rules and regulations for many countries in the world, and the new experimental feature, as of this writing, that allows GPT 4 to browse the web for something that it doesn't know yet, can provide a very useful interpreter for rules and regulations, even analyzing certain cases in determining whether a certain situation is within the established rules and norms.
- **Q&A**. Another great application is for ChatGPT to think out Q&A's for a particular scenario, text or body of knowledge. Users just need to enter a descriptive text regarding the object of analysis, and it will generate any number of Q&A's that can be used to clarify anything for students or the public in general.

As stated earlier, providing a list or taxonomy of possible uses and applications of generative AI is a futile exercise, since the possibilities are endless and creative teachers were passionate about learning we continuously find new uses in terms of making learning more engaging and interactive. As these applications become more powerful, update their databases and present new features, and despite the risks that we have already mentioned, the truly constitute what can be a formidable learning revolution, the one that we have been waiting for far too long.

## Summary

*Applications of AI in Math and Science:*

- Numeric problem solving with multiple methods
- Integration with complex mathematical platforms
- Science and Math word problems tackled in-depth
- Exam-oriented practice and test question generation
- Laboratory simulations for hands-on experience
- Creation of real-life based educational tasks
- Demonstrating practical uses of scientific and mathematical principles
- Generating perplexing data for critical thinking exercises
- Data analysis and statistical interpretation

*Anticipated Future Advancements:*

- Image input for non-textual data learning
- Real-time sensor data analysis

*Generative AI in History and Role-Playing:*

- Simulating dialogues with historical or current figures
- Crafting imaginative interactions between historical personalities
- Reanalyzing current events with a historical lens
- Active student participation in historical scenario reenactments

*Social Emotional Learning (SEL) via AI:*

- Tailored story creation for moral learning
- Role-play for problem-solving practice
- Emotional assistance under supervision
- Generation of reflective scenarios and cases
- Emotion recognition for empathy development
- Mindfulness and stress management guidance
- Digital citizenship and online behavior lessons
- Simulating conflict resolution for skills practice

*AI in Sports and Nutrition:*

- Personalized fitness and nutrition planning
- Progress tracking tools and datasheets
- Personalized diet plans and injury prevention information

*Generic Applications of Generative AI:*

- Negotiation, conflict resolution, and mystery role-plays
- Case study generation with reflective prompts
- Virtual travel and cultural exploration
- Time-travel simulations for contextual learning
- Test preparation and knowledge feedback
- Legal interpretation and case analysis
- Topic-specific Q&A session generation

*Prompts and applications*

Math and science
- Solve the following numeric problem - any math or science problem, with the only limitation that, for the time being, ChatGPT cannot accept images, surely soon to be upgraded.
- Explain each step in detail.
- Explain xxx step in greater detail.
- Write a similar problem to the one Justin third, for me to practice. Write separately the solution with explanations. (This can be customized by asking the system to include another topic, make it more simple or more complex, and give it any specification that the teacher or the student might require)
- Simulate experimental results for the following situation. Write a question or problem that students have to solve based on the data, together with a detailed solution.
- Write a problem that includes the following concepts xxxxx and that involves the following type of situation… Include the solution with a detailed explanation of each step.
- Give real-life applications of the following concept…. Provide explanations and concepts that are at the level of xxxx graders.
- Find historical events and examples for the following concept xxxx
- Generate a set of data for the following experiment… Be sure to include at least one item that

is out of range, one that is erroneous, and provide possible explanations for each.

Simulated interactive situations

- I want you to simulate the following scenario:...... I will be xxx, please answer my questions as if you were xxx.
- Reenact the following historical event:.... I want to engage in a dialogue with ... To try to solve ... situation. Change the historical outcome so that...
- Simulate a dialogue between ... and ... In which they discuss and debate about .... After the dialogue, allow me to ask them questions that all of them will answer.
- Answer my questions if you were... I will now conduct an interview with you.
- What would .... think about .... If they were alive now?

Social emotional learning

- Write a first-person narrative as if you were a person with ... Answer succeeding questions as that person.
- Create a story in which .... And when intervention by their friends results in .... (Generally a positive outcome)
- Answer as if you are a person that .... My questions afterwards are to try to help you improve your condition.
- Develop a case study in which the following conflict occurs... My students will then ask supplementary questions about the case so that they can engage in a conflict resolution exercise.
- I am a person that has the following condition

.... Please give me advice as to how to improve. NOTE: these, of course, is the most risky application of ChatGPT, and one that should be very carefully monitored by the teacher, making sure that it is tested before running it with the class, and, even in that case, ensuring that the teacher is present in case there are any unexpected or negative answers.
- I am currently undergoing a stressful situation because .... Please give me some mindfulness and meditation exercises that can help me cope. NOTE: this particular feature is probably more applicable to school induced stressful situations, such as exams, overworked students, academic pressure, etc., and only used with extreme caution for personal situations.
- I plan to post this on .... social network, let me know if it is appropriate and of any undesired consequences that this action might bring.

Sports and nutrition
- I am a xxx -year-old with xxx weight and height, I am in xxx physical condition, and I would need a fitness program to xxx (objective here, which could be from running a marathon to losing weight to becoming stronger). Develop the fitness plan over a period of xxx days. I have access to .... Describe here whether there are open spaces, whether that allows outdoor exercising, gym facilities, etc.
- Similarly, after entering personal information and any health or allergic conditions, develop a mail program for xxx days within a data budget of xxx. was generated by ChatGPT, the meal program can be personalized to any extent, such as not having access to certain ingredients, or not liking certain types of foods.

Needless to say, this can include gluten intolerance, vegan and vegetarian, or any other dietary preferences.
- I am a person who .... Describe injury, or any other physical situation here. Design and injury prevention or rehabilitation program including exercises that I can do before and after ... (Include here any competitive sport or activity that the person engages in regularly)
- There is the following situation in the game of... Explain whether this is within the rules or not and why.
- I plan to start .... (Describe physical activity or sport here). Provide me with a list of equipment that I must purchase together with personalized recommendations... (After entering personal data and physical measurements).
- I am in.... (Location) suggest an adequate route for jogging, walking, trails, etc. specify length and level of difficulty.

Other generic applications
- Create an escape room situation including the following concepts ... And involving the following skills... Make sure that all materials are easily accessible and within a low budget.
- Create a case study for the following situation: ....., Involving the following concepts...     Develop a series of questions that students may serve in order to understand and explore the resolution of this case study.
- Imagine that we are currently transported to... (Location) create a restaurant menu and a schedule of cultural events in that city.
- Write a detailed description of what you would find in a street in.... Without providing any data so

GABRIEL RSHAID

> that students can try to figure out where it is. Write an answer key and some hints that we can give students for them to try to guess the location. Include the following elements in the description - for example, cultural expressions, an item of food that is observed has been advertised on the window a restaurant, etc.
> - Imagine that we are living in (location) in (year). Write a description of the day the life of a person, together with places they can go to, events they attend, any issues they may encounter. Write questions for students to engage in further research on that historical time.
> - Given the following situation .... Explain whether it is within existing norms of regulations and why.
> - Develop a series of Q&A/FAQ for the following text/topic.

## Activity

This is what ChatGPT was asked to do:

Create a problem for fifth-graders to solve where they are confronted with a crime scene, and based on some of the clues and the problem they have to solve the mystery. The problem should involve applying math skills such as formulating and solving of simple equations, basic knowledge about chemical reactions and states of matter, and some cultural references that require them to perform research and learn about them. All the data needed to solve the problem should be contained in the text. Make sure that the text only includes a detailed description of the facts, but do not include any hints that might have the students solve the problem.

And here is the answer:

Title: "The Mystery of the Vanishing Necklace"

In the small town of Berryville, the local librarian, Mrs. Riley, was heartbroken to discover her precious diamond necklace missing from its usual spot in an antique wooden box. This wasn't just any necklace; it was an heirloom passed down from a distant relative in Egypt, filled with historical and sentimental value.

The room was airtight, with two windows and one door, all locked from the inside. Fresh snow dusted one window's sill. An empty glass beaker, a used packet of baking soda, and an empty vinegar bottle sat on a desk, droplets of a neutral liquid scattered around. A ruler lay on the desk, its shadow under the window light stretching to 12 feet.

Mrs. Riley's house was situated 60 feet away from "Old Ben", a majestic oak tree that towered at 120 feet. Intriguingly, a trail of footprints led from the base of the tree to the study's window. A peculiarly knotted rope was found dangling from one of the tree's branches.

The police found a note in Arabic hidden inside the antique wooden box that read:

"أنا أحب الذهب والألماس، ولكن الثقافة أكثر من ذلك."

Three individuals had visited Mrs. Riley on the previous day:

1. Mr. Parker, a long-time friend, a retired science teacher who was known to tinker with home science experiments, but mainly focused on biology and botany. He was trying to learn Spanish in his free time.
2. Mrs. Green, a translator by profession, known to have proficiency in several languages, including Arabic. She also happened to be a patron of local

arts and culture. However, she had a long-standing fear of heights.
3. Mr. Hughes, a landscaping professional, known for his agility and climbing skills, often used in his work. He was always seen with ropes and other equipment, but wasn't known to have any particular interest in languages or chemistry.

The local police hope that solving these problems will help reveal the identity of the thief:
1. Use the shadow and the ruler to calculate the distance the thief climbed down from the tree to reach the window.
2. Explain why there's a liquid and droplets on the desk, and what their relationship with the baking soda and vinegar might be.
3. Translate and interpret the note found in the box.

Can the fifth graders of Berryville help the local police solve the mystery of the vanishing necklace?

Solution:
1. By using the ratio from the shadow of the ruler and the ruler's actual length, we can set up the equation:
   1. $1/12 = x/60$, which when solved gives $x = 5$. So, the window is 5 feet from the ground. The thief would have needed to climb down 120 feet - 5 feet = 115 feet.

   2. The students would recognize that baking soda and vinegar create a reaction that results in carbonic acid, which quickly breaks down into water and carbon dioxide gas. The remaining liquid in the beaker is the result of this reaction,

> and the droplets on the desk are remnants of the fizzing reaction that occurred when the thief mixed these two substances together, likely creating a distraction.
>
> 3. The note translates to: "I love gold and diamonds, but culture more than that." This suggests that the thief didn't steal the necklace for its material value, but for its cultural significance.
>
> Based on the findings, the thief is likely to be Mr. Hughes. Despite him not being known for his interest in languages or chemistry, the necessity to climb down the tree and possibly tie the knot on the rope points towards him. As for the reaction and the note, he could have potentially received help or done enough research to execute the crime.

Needless to say, ChatGPT allows for the teacher to ask for multiple iterations and variations of the problem in question, changing part of the plot, making it more or less subtle, including more or less clues, and so on. This is a truly amazing feature, and anybody who has dabbed at creating engaging real-life problems knows how hard it is to develop hypothetical real-life interesting scenarios that are appropriate for certain age or grade level and that include the concepts required.

# MULTIMEDIA EXPRESSION

As technological developments progressed and many more applications were available for general use and their application to education, one of the areas in which schools made very little progress was that of multimedia expression. While multimedia remains the favored medium among children and teenagers, it is possible that a subconscious defense of traditional literacy skills continues to prevail, preventing more diversified modes of expression. Perhaps due to teachers lacking training in areas like graphic design and video editing, an essential part of contemporary communication, students are often graduating without basic proficiency in cutting-edge digital software. This deficit exists even though these tools provide an invaluable platform for multimedia self-expression.

## AI applications for image generation

As AI applications started to be deployed, one of the features that immediately caught the public eye was the possibility of generating images, and, subsequently, presentations and videos almost magically.

In effect, AI generated images have been around for a while, but improvements in processing power and generative AI have resulted in breathtaking output, even generating many a controversy regarding the ethics and validity of AI generated images, which came to the surface when, recently, an AI generated image as in obtained first prize in a Digital Art contest.

## AI generated images

The application is very simple and straightforward: user generated prompts, to the greatest level of detail possible, including styles and types of images, can generate a variation of AI images that can be re-tweaked, modified, and reinterpreted to the user's whims.

This constitutes the ultimate dream for aspiring artists, as the instrumental aspects of generating visual art are left to the AI, which does a very good job all of it, and the users´ artistic touch in terms of their expression consists in generating the prompts that most faithfully express their artistic intention.

## Tutorial for Writing Prompts for AI Image Generators

AI image generators can produce a range of visual styles, from photorealistic imagery to abstract art and even mimicking certain artistic styles. How you craft your prompts can greatly influence the end results.

1. Be Descriptive:

AI image generators work best with rich, detailed language. Try to detail the colors, shapes, and arrangement of elements.

Example:

Basic: "A cat."

Descriptive: "A fluffy, orange tabby cat lounging on a sunlit windowsill."

2. Define the Artistic Style or Realism Level:

AI can mimic various artistic styles, from Van Gogh's impressionism to Escher's surrealism. You can also request photorealistic images.

Example:

Impressionist style: "A vibrant cityscape in the style of Van Gogh's Starry Night."

Photorealistic: "A photorealistic image of a majestic snow-capped mountain against a clear blue sky."

### 3. Use Keywords for Different Genres:

Certain keywords will direct the AI towards specific genres. For example, "surreal" or "fantasy" can push the image toward the imaginative, while "modern" or "minimalistic" will yield a different style.

Example:

Surreal: "An alien planet with blue vegetation under a surreal purple sky."

Modern: "A modern minimalist living room with a large, white couch."

### 4. Consider Scale and Perspective:

You can play with size and perspective in your prompts to create interesting and innovative images.

Example:

"An ant's view of a towering sunflower in a lush garden."

### 5. Set a Mood or Atmosphere:

Adding mood descriptors can help set a specific tone or atmosphere for your image.

Example:

"A cozy, dimly lit library on a rainy day."

6. Combine Unusual Elements:

AI image generators excel at combining elements that wouldn't typically go together, resulting in unique and imaginative images.

Example:

"A cheetah running at full speed on the surface of Mars."

Variations:

Feel free to experiment with different prompts. Even slight changes in wording can produce diverse results. For example, "A tranquil pond at dusk" might yield a different result than "A serene pond at sunset."

By understanding how to write prompts and what keywords to use, you can fully utilize AI image generators to create a wide range of images, from photorealistic renderings to abstract or stylized compositions. Enjoy exploring the possibilities!

## Ethical issues

AI image generation, particularly with deep learning techniques, raises several ethical concerns. Here is a summary of the key issues associated with AI image generation:

- **Misuse and Misrepresentation**: AI-generated images can be misused for various purposes, including spreading misinformation, creating fake identities, or generating misleading content. This raises concerns about the potential for fraud, identity theft, and the manipulation of visual information.
- **Privacy and Consent**: AI image generation techniques can generate realistic images of people who may not have given their consent or even exist. This

poses privacy risks and challenges the notion of consent in image usage, potentially infringing upon an individual's rights and personal boundaries.

- **Deepfakes and Non-consensual Content**: Deepfakes refer to AI-generated media, including images and videos, that manipulate or superimpose faces onto existing content, often without the subject's consent. This technology has the potential for malicious use, such as revenge porn, defamation, or political manipulation, undermining trust and causing harm to individuals and society.
- **Bias and Stereotypes**: If the training data used for AI image generation contains biases or stereotypes, the generated images may perpetuate those biases. This can reinforce societal inequalities and discriminatory practices, especially when it comes to sensitive attributes like race, gender, or appearance.
- **Ownership and Intellectual Property**: AI-generated images raise questions about ownership and intellectual property rights. Determining who owns the generated content, especially when it involves repurposing existing images or artwork, becomes challenging and may require legal frameworks to address these issues.
- **Authenticity and Trust**: The proliferation of AI-generated images can erode trust in visual media, making it harder to distinguish between real and manipulated content. This can have far-reaching consequences in journalism, public discourse, and evidence authentication, impacting trust in the digital landscape.
- **Psychological and Emotional Impact**: Realistic AI-generated images can have psychological and emotional effects on individuals. They may lead to emotional distress, harassment, or invasion of privacy if used to create explicit, abusive, or harmful content.

## Presentations, social media and other multimedia

Similarly, a whole suite of applications have emerged that can directly generate, through AI, presentations, social media posts stories, not only in terms of the artistic creation but also incorporating the already related power of AI into generating content for them.

These applications allow for users to later edit and tweak both style as well as content, and, as we have seen with the many text to speech engines that are in existence, AI generated voices can read them out, thus delivering a whole package.

The ease of use and quality of these applications will undoubtedly improve over time, and the same lingering question that we will attempt to answer applies to all of these expressions and content generation: are they legitimate human expressions or the fact that the brunt of the work is carried out by an AI powered algorithm detracts from this being a genuine creation?

## Videos and digital animation.

Albeit if in their early stages, AI powered applications are also starting to dabble in video and animation generation, starting from prompts or detailed ideas and transforming them into videos of, for the time being, short duration, but this is to be expected given the technical difficulty of the feature being attempted.

For the time being, video generated by AI relies on stored clips, which are matched with the storyline created by the user and artificially generated voiceovers of the same type that are used for text-to-speech applications. In many cases, it is a best attempt, for the time being, and following the story, content or theme provided by the user.

Ad hoc AI generated digital animation still faces a similar challenge, in that generating AI animated scenes, even to a low risk level of detail, is still beyond current capabilities of regular computers, not to mention that eventually transferring them in real time over the Internet would hog enormous amounts of bandwidth.

But, as we all know, this may be superseded in the future by faster processors and increased bandwidth, thus not making it out of the question that, eventually, we will have software that can generate on-the-fly 3-D detailed digital animations that can be tweaked, edited and redone to materialize our creativity and imagination.

Deep fakes already embody this technology, by replacing digitally scanned images of faces into existing videos or ad hoc rendered scenes, presenting us with the challenge of deciding whether media is to be trusted at all, and when an image or video is part of some items of news whether it can be trusted for it to be legitimate or not.

## Implications

Many of the implications that were analyzed in the previous paragraph regarding AI generated images apply and are augmented when it comes to animation and video. If AI generated video clips, for example, became accessible to even casual users with ease, and they attain a level of realism that makes them indistinguishable from reality, our perception of media reality can be forever altered, rendering, literally, media impossible to believe unless their authenticity is proved conclusively in some way.

## Yes, but is it art?

I have personally witnessed discussions involving artists in the digital art community, expressing concerns about the validity of utilizing AI generated images and whether they can be considered art or not. There is of course, no right or wrong answer to this profound question, but it is interesting to analyze some of the arguments in favor and against AI generated images since they are burdened into deeper discussions regarding content and knowledge in general.

The perennial question of what constitutes art is far beyond our analysis, but, in the case of AI generated creations, it is very interesting to analyze what ultimately constitutes the artists´ genuine input and form of expression. Pixar is a great example. At this age and time, nobody would dare question that many Pixar movies are sublime expression of creativity in cinema, and even though these are 3-D computer-generated animations, the computers themselves are just considered mere mechanical devices that are tweaked, with great effort and ingenuity, to produce the artist´s desired outcomes.

Let's imagine for an instant that a prompt based AI application is able to generate quality 3-D animations just by detailed text based interactions. Would the fact that the use of such a system is far more simple than the painstaking hours and computer processing power that are invested in generating 3-D animations at this stage make it less acceptable as an art form than a Pixar movie?

The key, as in anything else that we consider regarding the use of these AI systems has to do with redefining what constitutes the unique mark of a content creator, or, in this case, an artist, whether interacting via text based prompts with a generative AI application that can create videos or animations is not considered enough of an artistic expression to warrant it being considered as an art form.

As with learning, the ultimate judge is the reason why we create in the first place. In my personal opinion, it does not matter whether a machine has generated art or it has been handcrafted by human, as long as it produces the desired aesthetic effect and can evoke the depth of feeling and artistic appreciation that makes art one of the quintessential human passions.

And, anticipating a future discussion, it may very well be similar for the generation of new knowledge and content.

## Summary

*Education and Multimedia:*

- Schools are behind in multimedia expression despite technology advancements.
- Traditional literacy skills overshadow multimedia modes of expression.
- Lack of teacher training in modern communication mediums like graphic design and video editing.
- Students graduate without proficiency in essential digital software.

*AI in Image Generation:*

- AI applications are advancing in image generation with a variety of visual styles.
- User prompts can direct AI to produce diverse images which are adjustable.
- AI benefits aspiring artists by handling instrumental aspects of visual art creation.

*Writing Prompts for AI:*

- Detailed, descriptive prompts yield better results.
- Specifying artistic style can lead to photorealistic images.

- Keywords can guide AI towards specific genres.
- Creative manipulation of scale, perspective, mood, and element combinations can produce innovative images.

Ethical Issues with AI Image Generation:
- Misuse and misrepresentation risks with AI-generated images.
- Privacy and consent concerns, especially with realistic human images.
- Potential for deepfakes and non-consensual content.
- Risk of AI perpetuating existing biases and stereotypes.
- Unclear intellectual property rights and eroding trust in visual media.
- Potential psychological impacts of realistic AI-generated images.

AI in Multimedia:
- AI can generate presentations, social media posts, and stories.
- These applications offer editing options for style and content.
- AI-generated voices can narrate these creations.
- Questions remain about the authenticity of AI-generated content.

AI in Video and Animation:
- AI is beginning to explore video and animation generation.
- AI videos currently rely on stored clips, user-created storylines, and AI voiceovers.
- Real-time AI animation faces challenges due to computing power and bandwidth limitations.
- Deepfakes pose issues of media trust.

*Implications:*

- Ethical issues of AI-generated images intensify with animation and video.
- If AI videos become accessible and realistic, it could alter our perception of media reality.

*AI and Art:*

- Debates exist about the legitimacy of AI-generated images as art.
- Questions surround what constitutes the artist's genuine input.
- The use of AI in creating videos or animations is under scrutiny.
- The key debate is about what constitutes a unique artist.
- The ultimate measure may be whether AI art can evoke depth of feeling and appreciation.

# ADVANCED APPLICATIONS

We live in an era marked by exponential technological advancements. The widespread use of the Internet, enhanced connectivity allowing real-time audio and video communication globally, virtual and augmented reality, big data, and smartphones are just a few examples of disruptive technologies that have radically changed our lives over the past 30 years.

However, nothing compares to the sudden emergence of ChatGPT and other generative artificial intelligence applications. From the outset, even the first version released to the market displayed amazing capabilities—a mature, user-friendly product accessible to the general public. Furthermore, and this is the focus of this section, new applications and innovations that extend the features and capabilities of ChatGPT and other AI systems are being introduced literally every day.

Despite the likelihood of this information becoming outdated soon, we will attempt to explore some of the most advanced capabilities recently incorporated into ChatGPT, with a focus on their application in education.

## ChatGPT Plus Version

I have no commercial interest or affiliation with OpenAI, the company that created ChatGPT, but I can´t recommend enough obtaining a paid subscription, GPT Plus. This version enables the majority of the advanced applications we will subsequently discuss.

It also runs on the GPT-4 language model, significantly more advanced and accurate than GPT-3.5, and trained with many more parameters—almost an order of magnitude more than the free version.

The current cost is USD 20 per month, and while the impact of this subscription varies from country to country, it doesn't seem out of range for a school or educational organization. It likely represents the best investment in education for a school, as it also offers unlimited training possibilities for its teachers through interaction, trial, and error.

## Web Access through Bing

As mentioned earlier, OpenAI has a strategic alliance with Microsoft, one of its main investors, providing infrastructure and server software for its operation.

Therefore, it's not surprising that Bing, Microsoft's search engine, is the service provider for extending the system's limited knowledge. While the free version of ChatGPT, limited now to January 2022, has a closed knowledge database, which is one of its main limitations since it not only lacks access to current events, but also any data or knowledge not included in its training database does not exist for ChatGPT, with the risk that its illusion of knowing everything makes us forget that it is a finite knowledge database.

This limitation has been overcome, as the current version now allows unlimited access to the web through Bing. Until the second week of November 2023, access to the Bing search option was explicit, so it was up to the user to decide whether to extend the system's capabilities with the search engine or limit it to the data already within the system.

OpenAI has just released the multimodal version to the public, meaning all these advanced features, except for the plugins, are now embedded within ChatGPT Plus, which, in turn, implies that the system now decides itself when to seek information.

From the user's point of view, and in its application in education, the knowledge database organically extends to cover everything available on the Internet, with its advantages and disadvantages.

On one hand, the system becomes slower when searching for information on the Internet, as this no longer depends on the speed of its server but rather on the two-way Internet connection with the user, and limits the capacity to process that information to a much smaller volume than it has accumulated.

It is undeniable that, as ChatGPT's new feature is used, the system will improve in terms of speed and criteria for accessing the Internet, but, undoubtedly, it represents a significant advance.

## Image Recognition

Another extremely interesting feature is the ability to start any conversation and learning interaction with ChatGPT from an image. The system's image recognition capability is astonishing and can lead to fascinating applications in the world of education.

The system works very simply; you can upload any type of image in the formats commonly used on computers, and ChatGPT will be able to recognize it and start processing from the information obtained from that image, continuing as if textual information had been entered.

Some application examples include:

- **OCR (Optical Character Recognition).** ChatGPT now recognizes text with a very high level of precision, what was once limited to very specialized software can be directly incorporated by ChatGPT. Just upload a handwritten text, a photograph of a book, or any other image that contains text, in whole or in part, and ChatGPT can convert it into a digitally usable text format.
- **Reading of plans and schematics.** Another amazing capability of the system is its ability to interpret plans, sketches, and diagrams, even reading measurements and calculating areas or making any subsequent projection based on the image entered.
- **Contextual information from the image.** This is also a very useful feature, from recognizing an animal breed to a plant species, or asking for a recipe from a photo of a meal we upload. ChatGPT can interpret with a very high level of accuracy any image we upload and act as if it were our eyes but with much more extensive and greater knowledge than we can possess.
- **Create code from an image.** It is now also possible to generate design or programming code that reproduces a scheme or diagram we upload, which represents a potentially astonishing capability, knowing how difficult it is to go from an image to a computational design.
- **Mathematical modeling.** ChatGPT can also generate equations and mathematical models from graphs or any other information provided in image form.

As it can be seen, the applications are almost unlimited, left to the user's imagination, but it is very important to clarify something: the system is designed to prevent any manipulation or facial recognition, so there is a very strict limitation on images of people, as, for now, the system refuses to process beyond generic descriptions.

## DALLE-3 – Image Generation

DALLE-3 is one of the most advanced artificial intelligence image generation systems, entirely developed by OpenAI. Now, quite naturally for the user, it can create images of all kinds, as we saw in the image generation section.

What is novel about its incorporation into the ChatGPT interface is, of course, that it can be combined with any other generative process with the application, allowing, for example, images to be generated from the result of a search, solving a problem, or any other previous process that is concatenated within the chat. As we have also said, generating images requires an extensive trial-and-error process, and it is also advisable to look for tutorials for each of these applications, and DALLE-3 is no exception, to take full advantage of the different modalities, types of images generated, filters, styles, etc.

## Talking with ChatGPT

The possibility of speaking with ChatGPT, communicating directly through the microphone of our mobile device, is also available. Although it is a very simple application that does not modify the system's capabilities, its use represents a substantial step in terms of accessibility, especially for people with visual impairments, as well as the speed, practicality, and convenience of having an audio interface with the chat.

## Data Analysis

Perhaps the most powerful of these new applications, and one that has potentially unlimited effects and a huge impact on education, is what has been labelled Advanced Data Analysis.

This relatively new feature of ChatGPT allows the user to attach a file into the system, of any nature, whether it is a text, spreadsheet, or any other information, and, however long and complex it may be, by providing the system with the appropriate information, it will be able to process and respond to queries and requests from the user.

The process involves the following steps:

- Upload the file to the system.
- Develop clear step-by-step instructions that allow ChatGPT to understand the data structure, chapters, or sections into which the text is divided. While the system can do this on its own, a lot of time is saved and confusion avoided by giving detailed instructions to the chat so that it can perform a more advanced interpretation of the data or information.
- Ideally, request that the system perform a simple analysis of the data, which can be easily verified by the user, to check that the system has read and properly incorporated the information to be analyzed.

Once it is verified that the system has understood the data structure, various types of analysis can be requested, both mathematical and statistical, creating graphs, diagrams, inferences, applying ChatGPT's language engine indiscriminately to these data.

We must also point out an advanced capability of the system, that of generating documents in formats such as doc, PDF, or a spreadsheet, that can subsequently be downloaded.

Some possible applications to education include:

- **Analysis of standardized test results**. Many educational leaders are tasked to make presentations to whatever their supervisors are, for example, regarding the results of international exams or standardized tests. By simply structuring the data adequately, the system can calculate averages,

correlations, weighted averages, perform statistical inferences, ranking of the best subjects, teacher effects, etc.
- **Review of lesson plans according to a defined rubric.** Another perhaps less attractive responsibility of educational leaders is academic supervision, which includes reviewing lesson plans, suggest improvements, and, in general, provide appropriate feedback to teachers. By generating a rubric that defines what is sought in a lesson plan or school planning or curriculum, the system can analyze what a teacher has developed, and provide detailed observations and feedback based on that rubric, which can be generated in a separate document that can be handed directly to the teacher.
- **Analysis of school management system data.** School management systems usually provide a huge amount of data, which is very difficult to process. Having a very advanced assistant to generate correlations and inferences, it is possible, for example, to relate academic results to attendance, the effectiveness of certain teachers, or even to look for relationships between variables that apparently do not have too much link between them.
- **Keyword Search for Generating Strategic Insights**: One of the eternal dilemmas of education is how to find qualitative measures, as quantitative measurements, such as standardized evaluations, are intrinsically challenged in terms of their rigidity and not measuring the process. This type of tool allows for examining lesson plans, school curriculums, etc., in relation to a series of terms that can be defined as a kind of dictionary of what is desired to generate in the school, formative evaluation, critical thinking, and even quantify to what extent this occurs in the activities that teachers develop.

- **Correcting Student Assignments**: Perhaps the most historically desired application, almost like an eternal prayer, is now within reach of educators: the ability to generate automatic corrections of work done by students, and to do so with a level of detail and personalization that is unreachable even for the most dedicated of teachers. The following is the procedure to achieve this desired objective:
    - Upload, in a file, the assignment, question, work, or task assigned to the students.
    - Subsequently, indicate to ChatGPT the reference, if there is one, regarding the task, for example, a video, article, resource, or any other source of information necessary to be able to resolve it.
    - Ideally, upload a file with the rubric developed by the teacher - or, even better, by ChatGPT itself - that would be used to evaluate the task in question.
    - Either in a single file, ideally, to save time, or one by one, start uploading the files with the students' responses.
    - Instruct ChatGPT to do the following:
        - The first file I have uploaded is a task that students must complete, the second includes the reference rubric, and the last file or series of files are the students' tasks.
        - Rewrite the file or files with the students' tasks including, for each of the responses, the detailed correction in italics on the same document, without changing what the students have written, only adding in each response the suggestions and feedback, seeking to be constructive,

formative evaluation.
- If it was also the objective, ChatGPT can assign a score based on a rubric, as seen before, either created by the system itself or by the teacher.

  As we have seen on repeated occasions, it is difficult for even a system as advanced as ChatGPT to provide the desired response in a first instance, but after a few integrations, we can generate the mechanism to automate this process.

  Regarding whether we are legitimately adding value as educators, on the one hand, the detail, personalization, quantity, and quality of feedback, once the teacher manages to calibrate the system's response, is incomparable to what any human can do, and, additionally, the ability to download or delegate this task to the system frees up time for the teacher to be able to work individually with their students and, there, indeed, add a lot of value in those types of personal interactions.

- **Document Digitization**: The capability previously mentioned of ChatGPT to be able to read images and transform these images into digitally processed text is extremely useful when it comes to digitizing the content of documents, as it is very common in schools to have either historical documents, or records that can be easily digitally stored from this possibility.

- **Creating New Files of All Types**: One of the most interesting features of the new multimodal GPT4 is that the system now incorporates the ability to generate files, whether Google documents, spreadsheets, PDFs, and presentations, with which the output of the generated process can be directly channeled into a document. The system also features the ability to add certain design features, which must be, more than anything, evaluated with trial and error, such as modern design, elegant, adding logos, etc.

It is impossible, of course, to try to generate a taxonomy, however minimalist it may be, of the applications that can be achieved from this new feature of ChatGPT, bearing in mind, in addition, that, undoubtedly, it will rapidly improve as the weeks and months go by. However, the list above more or less covers the generic applications and can serve as a good starting point.

## *Plugins*

What emerged as a timid phenomenon a few months after ChatGPT was developed, has already reached incredible dimensions, with the incorporation of modules from other providers, which allow connecting the ChatGPT engine to their own databases and systems to generate artificial intelligence applications that are directly focused on certain areas.

There are, literally, as of the date of generating this text, November 2023, approximately 1500 plugins available, making it almost impossible to make recommendations, with the addition that some of them have become obsolete with the new features offered by ChatGPT.

For example, one of the most used was those that allowed access in real-time to links on the Internet, a capability that the system already possesses, or reading and analyzing PDFs, which has also been incorporated into the standard features of the Plus version.

The range of applications of the plugins is as diverse as it is varied, including for planning trips (although these are not probably up to expectations yet) generating diagrams of all kinds, connection with e-commerce engines, diets, nutrition, recommendations, academic searches, specific searches in video, etc.

Quite recently, OpenAI has also announced that it will be launching its own App Store, taking the concept of the plugin a step further, with what is believed to be standalone applications that incorporate the ChatGPT engine and not as an added module that must be explicitly selected as is currently the case with plugins.

## The Future of Artificial Intelligence

In less than a year since the appearance of artificial intelligence applications, we have already seen changes of a very considerable magnitude, new applications, and advances almost daily. This makes it almost a sterile exercise to try to predict what changes or advances these systems will feature in the immediate future.

It is possible, however, to try to foresee the general direction in which these possible advances will be oriented. As a first measure, an even more intuitive interface with the user will be generated, improving what already exists in terms of image reading, voice interface, and, conversely, the system's response through the generation of graphics, images, audio, and video.

It is also expected that the generation of videos and animations with a photo-realistic level will improve significantly in quality, in fact, there are applications right now that generate images indistinguishable from a digital photograph in 4K, starting from text descriptions and making them a reality in auto-generated images.

In that order, it is also very possible that these systems greatly improve their interpretation of the commands that are given for the generation of images and videos. It needs to be remembered that the system can only interpret what is written, so it will always have to do with the clarity and precision with which the user can generate the prompts, but without a doubt, the personalization of the generation of images will be more advanced from going developing the user's own "artistic" style.

Another area where the system is expected to improve is in the integration, almost in real time, with other data that are not its own, being able to cover, for example, large volumes of external data and apply the same system architecture to its analysis and generation of response.

We will also see, most likely, the intuitive integration of these systems into humanoids and other robots that, from this very advanced architecture, will be able to make the long-postponed dream of these cybernetic companions who can assist people, keep them company, and also, why not, provide entertainment.

## Summary:

*Technological Development and ChatGPT*

- Exponential Growth Context: In the last three decades, technologies such as the Internet, virtual and augmented reality, and smartphones have significantly transformed our everyday life.
- Revolution with ChatGPT and AI: ChatGPT, since its first version, has shown remarkable capabilities, offering a mature and accessible product for the public. Generative AI is updated daily, expanding its capabilities.

*Advanced Capabilities of ChatGPT*

- Focus on Education: The latest additions to ChatGPT are investigated, especially in how they can be applied in the educational sector.

*The Plus Version of ChatGPT*

- Substantial Improvements: The Plus version, powered by GPT-4, offers accuracy and advanced capabilities superior to previous versions.
- Cost and Accessibility: At a price of 20 dollars a month, this version is presented as a valuable and accessible

investment for educational institutions.

*Access to the Web through Bing*

- Collaboration with Microsoft: The integration with Bing allows ChatGPT to access up-to-date information from the web, overcoming the limitations of closed database systems.
- Innovation in Web Search: The latest version allows for automatic web searches, significantly expanding the system's knowledge reach.

*Image Recognition*

- Versatility in Recognition: ChatGPT can now interpret images for OCR, read plans, provide contextual information, create code, and mathematically model from images.
- Ethical Limitations: There is a strict policy against facial recognition to prevent manipulation or invasion of privacy.

*DALLE-3*

- AI Image Generation: Integrated into ChatGPT, it allows for the creation of images based on previous information and analysis, opening a range of creative possibilities.

*Spoken Interaction with ChatGPT*

- Audio Interface: The possibility of interacting with ChatGPT through voice improves accessibility, especially useful for users with visual difficulties.

*Data Analysis*

- Advanced Functionality: ChatGPT now allows users to upload and analyze complex data. This feature is particularly useful in the educational field, where data collection and analysis play a crucial role.
- Types of Files and Data: The system is capable of processing various file formats, such as text and spreadsheets. This allows educators and school administrators to analyze

a wide range of data, from exam results to school management data.

*Customized Instructions*

- For effective analysis, users must provide clear and detailed instructions to ChatGPT. These instructions help the system understand the structure and context of the data, facilitating more accurate analysis.

*Analysis and Queries*

- Once the system understands the data structure, it can perform a variety of analyses, such as mathematical calculations, statistics, generation of graphs and diagrams, and inferences based on the provided data.

*Validation and Continuous Improvement*

- Users should initially verify the accuracy of ChatGPT's analyses to ensure that the data has been interpreted correctly. With continued use, the system improves its accuracy and effectiveness in data analysis.

*Document Generation*

- A notable feature is ChatGPT's ability to generate documents in common formats like .doc, PDF, or spreadsheets, which can include the results of data analysis. This is useful for report presentation and studies.

*Educational Applications:*

- Analysis of Exam Results: Educators can use ChatGPT to analyze standardized test results, identifying trends, averages, and correlations.
- Academic Supervision: Allows for the review and analysis of lesson plans according to established rubrics, providing objective and constructive feedback to teachers.
- School Management: Assists in the analysis of school management system data, such as correlating academic

results with attendance or teacher effectiveness.
- Keyword Search: Facilitates the search for key terms in educational documents to obtain strategic insights and quantify qualitative aspects of education.
- Automated Task Correction: ChatGPT can automate the correction of student assignments, providing detailed and personalized feedback based on a predefined rubric.

*Plugins*

- Diversity and Functionality: With a large number of plugins available, the functionalities of ChatGPT are expanded, although some may have become obsolete with recent updates.

*The Future of Artificial Intelligence*

- Anticipated Advances: Greater integration of AI in intuitive interfaces, advanced multimedia content generation, and the incorporation of AI into robots for various functions are expected.

# ETHICAL AND SOCIAL IMPLICATIONS

As AI systems become more ubiquitous, integrated with other devices, and transparently omnipresent in underlying plugins for existing applications, their impact will not only be paramount in education, but they will very much alter the way we live and relate to each other, both individually as well as in our societal roles.

The ever-increasing influence that AI and other technological developments will have in our lives far transcends the applications to learning and places us educators in the always unenviable position to be the ones have to decode these implications and try to harness them, if possible, for positive impact, or, at least, to mitigate any negative consequences they might have.

The integration of AI with some other recent developments, such as big data, augmented reality and advanced robots, including humanoids, pose some dire challenges for our students, who will have to grow up in a radically changed world, and one that will challenge not only their ability to function effectively in society but also to redefine their humanity. And, once again, it will be up to us educators to make the best of this fascinating and also tantalizing scenario, even if we don't have a clearly defined pedagogy or rulebook to deal with it.

The sections that ensue will attempt to present some of the

main issues associated with current unexpected technological developments, and present some of the ethical dilemmas associated with their application to our everyday lives, so that motivate our students to reflect on these challenges and implications in ways that help them become critical and cognizant users of these new technologies. There will be more questions than answers, but, at this stage in technological and human evolution, it is probably more important to ask the right questions than to try to provide answers that may prove to be as elusive as they are uncertain.

In all of these cases, it is important that students learn, as part of their core curriculum, how many of these applications are developed and their inner workings, so as to be able to discern what their impact will be, and become critical consumers of current and imminent technology developments that will be ever more impactful in our lives.

## *Big Data*

Big data applications have been around for many years already, and have become even indistinguishable for end-users, who very naturally browse, for example, Amazon and follow up on automatic recommendations based on each user's unique profile as compared to hundreds of thousands of other customers who have made similar purchases. However, big data applications for education are not as well known or understood, even though they may have some very important consequences in the present and the future.

Big data refers to extremely large data sets that can be analyzed computationally to reveal patterns, trends, and associations. It often involves data collection, storage, analysis, and visualization on a scale beyond the capacity of traditional databases. Its applications span various fields, from business intelligence and predictive modeling to scientific research and policy-making. As bandwidth became a lot faster and processing powers increased exponentially, as per Moore's law, big data applications are not only reserved to large corporate databases, but can be organic, real-time, and live on the Internet.

As big data is increasingly deployed across several fields, it is starting to make an impact on education. I was recently in a university that tracks heat maps for student devices, that is, based on the IP or MAC address of each device, and correlating that information with what the Internet routers can supply, it can easily track where students have been during their day at school.

Administrators at this university told me about how they use this heat map information, in what is a direct application of big data. When the system detects that two devices are proximal to each other during a substantial part of the day, it supposes that the owners of those devices are either best friends or a couple. If after a certain period of time, the devices are no longer together, and go mostly about their separate ways, throughout the school day at the university, the new inference is that either the friends or the couple have broken up. They then immediately give notice to their counseling department so that they can summon, separately, the students in question, and, without necessarily referring to the breakup, inquire after their well-being.

When asked whether this was ethical or not, the same administrators replied to me that it was all done in the best interests of the students involved, whilst also acknowledging that these emotional issues are one of the main causes of college dropout.

This anecdote only serves to emphasize the tremendous ethical implications, both existing and potential, the use of big data in education. Some of them are:

- **Privacy and Data Protection**: Schools and educational institutions collect a vast amount of data on students. These data can include personal and sensitive information such as health records, family income,

and academic performance. There is a risk of misuse of this data if not properly protected, and also a potential for data breaches, as well as presenting a kind of intrinsic dilemma for policymakers and administrators and whether the data is used for any purposes in terms of pedagogical strategies or eventual interventions.
- **Consent**: It is essential to ensure that students, or their parents or guardians in the case of minors, understand what data is being collected, how it will be used, and to whom it might be disclosed. They should have the ability to give informed consent.
- **Equity**: Big data can be used to identify trends and make predictions about student performance, but it is important to ensure that these tools don't exacerbate existing inequalities. For example, predictive algorithms might unfairly disadvantage certain groups of students if they are based on biased data. As we have seen with some of the earlier models upon which generative AI systems were developed, part of the reinforcement process implies what is known as de-biasing these models, but that is probably beyond the reach of any educational institution.
- **Transparency**: The algorithms used to analyze big data are often complex and not easily understood by those without a technical background. This can lead to a lack of transparency about how decisions are being made, especially if they affect the student´s academic life in any respect.
- **Data Ownership**: There are questions about who owns the data that is collected in an educational context. Is it the school, the student, or some third party? And since data is intrinsically valuable, especially big data, who would eventually have the right to benefit from the ownership of the data?
- **Use of Predictive Analytics**: The use of predictive

analytics in education can lead to ethical concerns, particularly if these tools are used to track students or make determinations about their future potential based on past performance. When it comes to teacher assignments, preventive interventions, or any other education measure that has implications on the students´ school experience, it is to be questioned to what extent these decisions can be made based on big data and predictive algorithms.

## AI-based adaptive systems for personalized learning

Some applications already exist and are being widely used that harness the positive power of AI for learning. With more emphasis on math, foreign language learning and reading, these applications start from a diagnostic test of each of the students, developing a cognitive profile for each of them, and presenting users with progressive exercises and challenges based on hundreds of thousands of data points that can help shape up an optimal learning experience based on a path that allows students to be both challenged and successful.

These applications deliver on the promise of personalized learning, and if they have a big repository of exercises and activities, the constant feedback obtained from user interaction, including time spent in each exercise, relative measures of success, errors, and so on, third grade way to accompany students amongst a learning path that gives them the best possible learning experience, together with a complete set of results and data reporting.

## The big transparency question

We have already touched upon what is known as the transparency problem, which becomes an issue with these very advanced large language model-based generative AI systems, which are as accurate as they are opaque, since their very complexity prevents even their programmers from known how a decision is arrived at.

These raises a profound question, which is at the center of the transparency issue: do people have the right to obtain explanations for any algorithmic decisions that are made on their behalf?

In our field of education, we can say that both students and parents may very well have the right to understand why any instructional or academic decisions are made by the school when based on predictive algorithms based on big data.

As the marriage of AI and big data becomes more commonplace, these issues will have greater importance, and even as we rely on the power and customization of AI systems to provide what is an attempt to deliver the best, personalized learning experience for students, some ethical issues are also raised regarding whether even diagnostic testing and cognitive profiles from adaptive systems are free from negative biases or perpetuating stereotypes.

## Implicit decisions made by AI systems.

As AI based systems become more prevalent and usable, they will become embedded into many everyday applications, and as we progressively become used to their omnipresence in many of the systems we use, it is hard to even detect that there are some decisions that are being made for us and that can be implicit in the use of the application.

A great example of one of these decisions has to do with self-driving cars. The algorithm behind the self-driving car not only needs to monitor, through sensors, real-time information about the context in order to provide the system with the guidance needed to be able to navigate traffic and safely drive the car, but it also needs to make certain decisions regarding the safety and security and potential scenarios that may occur.

The MIT Moral Machine (http://moralmachine.mit.edu/) is a wonderful online interactive site that presents some of the ethical dilemmas associated with the design of these algorithms, comparing them with a classical philosophical problem of the past, the Trolley Problem.

The Trolley Problem is a hypothetical moral dilemma in which a runaway trolley is headed towards five people tied to the tracks; you can pull a lever to divert it, but it will kill one person on the alternate track. The ethical dilemma arises from the conflict between consequentialism (the greatest good for the greatest number) and deontology (the belief in inherent rightness or wrongness of actions). This tests our intuition about the difference between actively causing harm (pulling the lever) and passively allowing harm (doing nothing).

MIT Moral Machine presents users with a similar problem, by asking users to make decisions on a number of scenarios whereby they need to assess situations in which the self-driving car may either put its own occupants in harm's way, by crashing against a barrier, or divert from the barrier and endanger or altogether kills some of the passersby that are crossing the street.

This faces us with, of course, the great moral dilemma that is increasingly present for programmers, who make decisions about even such extreme scenarios as the ones showcased on the site, which then proceeds to provide users with feedback on their decisions based on the hundreds of thousands of other answers in their database, in what is also an interesting application of big data.

This site is a great example for students to start familiarizing themselves with some of these decisions that are implicitly made by the AI systems, which have to incorporate all of these variables into their design, and as they provide, for example, guidance for weapons and even commercial aircraft, have to make certain decisions that are implicit in the process.

Not all cases are so extreme, and there are other many examples of algorithmic decisions that are embedded in AI-powered software that are present in our everyday lives, but it is a great primer for students to start to consider that not all is as automatic as it seems and that there are humans who design software and who make those decisions for users.

## *Augmented Reality*

The Google Glasses were an ill-fated gadget that was probably released long before the technology was mature, but it did serve to capture the public's imagination about the promise of augmented reality. In a nutshell, augmented reality works through some sensor, normally a camera, that can process and recognize images and provide, through an algorithm via a database or real-time access to the Internet, contextual information about the person's surroundings.

Smart glasses are now being marketed by other companies, and in various shapes and forms are making a comeback, basically functioning with a camera that once more interprets the surroundings, identifies objects and different entities in the reality that surrounds the person, and then as per an algorithm, provides some kind of information regarding what it has recognized.

This can be perfectly harmless when it comes to supplying information about a tourist attraction, or even recognizing an object and connecting with a product review, nutritional information about food we are about to consume, or any other data that helps the user make some informed decision or get more information about what they are experiencing at the moment.

The real ethical issues come into play when this is applied to persons. As image recognition improves and pattern recognition becomes more state-of-the-art, we are not far from the time when, like many movies show when they are trying to find the whereabouts of the suspect of a crime, faces are recognized and processed in real time.

This would imply that when somebody meets a person for the first time and they don't know them, the smart glasses may identify the person, go to the internet and provide information that it finds on the person even before you shake their hand (or bump fists in the post pandemic era...) and meet them for the first time.

This can have some dire implications, since for the first time, technology would interact in real time with our sensorial perceptions and generate algorithmic output that supplements our senses. It is bad enough that people have to live with their indelible digital footprint on the internet when somebody goes to find them on any search engine, or now on ChatGPT, but it's even worse if that will condition even spontaneous human interactions like meeting somebody for the first time.

This, of course, raises some profound ethical dilemmas about the right of a person to withhold information and not be recognizable by such a device, which would lead to an almost improbable faces blacklist if a person opted out of being identified by the system or else be very concerned about how other people could potentially get a first impression on them mostly from what can be found on them on the Internet.

## Social networks and privacy concerns.

The emergence of AI compounds what until now has been a dire issue in education, how students use social networks, privacy issues and safety online. Social network use and messaging apps have become widespread over the last few years, and more especially so with teenagers, who take to the online medium with complete ease of use and in a very natural way, in the same way as we engage in conversations.

For children and teenagers who grew up in a world where social networks were a very natural medium of communication, there are no antibodies when it comes to privacy concerns. So, once more, it is teachers and educators who need to provide some guidance in that respect.

There is a certain degree of naiveté when it comes to analyzing how social networks take our data and what they make of it. A few years back, a Netflix documentary, The Social Dilemma, portrayed this issue of how social networks take our data and, in a way, may shield us from reality by providing us with only the part of reality that we customize, based on our preferences, with the purported evil intention of selling ads to us.

However, in reality, the documentary itself is a masterpiece of viewer manipulation, incurring in the same actual crime that they seek to denounce, since they present a very skewed and partial version of reality. So much so, that the trailer for the documentary features a screen capture where a pretended user searches for "climate change" on Google and gets search engine results to the effect that climate change is a hoax, doesn't exist, etc., which of course is definitely not what actually happens when any of us do search for "climate change" on Google in real life.

This documentary notwithstanding, there are real issues concerning privacy, but students need to understand some of the underlying issues in what is, ultimately, a global market economy. Many of these messaging apps allow us almost unlimited bandwidth to store videos, engage in live audio and video calls, send unlimited images, and many other applications that are expensive to maintain, especially when it comes to thousands of millions of users as they have.

This, of course, is not an intrinsic human right and we should not expect that these companies are going to give this out for free just for the benefit of humanity, but rather to get something in return. Studies have proven that users are reticent to pay even small amounts for the use of these applications, so companies have to rely on the use of this data for commercial uses, selling them usually to companies that then miraculously appear on our feeds, selling us the very stuff that we were talking about a few minutes earlier.

What creeps us out for the justified fear that devices are listening to us, can, indeed, be very disturbing, but it is, in fact, none other than the monetization of a free application. And, in most cases, it is harmless, only providing us with choices for purchasing stuff that we may not need, but at the same time highly unlikely that it will impinge on our privacy or have any other detrimental consequences to ourselves.

This issue should not, by any means, be taken lightly and users should learn from a very early age how to deal with these privacy issues and understand what kind of data these social networks and messaging applications are taking from us, how it is being marketed and what purpose it's being used for.

As long as we are critical, cognizant users of these applications, the trade-off is each consumer's choice. Do we want to use the apps that are given to us for free with immense capabilities and allow us to remain connected at all times? Or would we rather opt out of them for the sake of privacy?

## The implicit bias problem.

A few years back, Harvard University released Harvard Project Implicit (https://implicit.harvard.edu/implicit/), a controversial social study using big data that analyzed response time to measure implicit biases in many sensitive areas.

Implicit bias refers to the attitudes or stereotypes that affect our understanding, actions, and decisions in an unconscious manner. These biases are involuntary and often something individuals are unaware of. Implicit biases can favor our own in-group (people who share characteristics with us) or hold prejudice against an out-group (people who are different from us). Importantly, these biases don't necessarily align with our declared beliefs, and can contradict them.

One of the key elements of Project Implicit is the Implicit Association Test (IAT), which is designed to measure the strength of a person's automatic association between mental representations of objects in memory. There are many versions of the IAT for different types of biases, such as race, gender, sexuality, etc.

Here's a basic example of how the IAT works: In a race-related IAT, participants might be asked to quickly categorize faces as Black or White, and words as positive or negative. If a participant more quickly associates White faces with positive words and Black faces with negative words, they would be said to have an implicit bias favoring Whites over Blacks.

At the end of each test, and users can run through various very sensitive issues, such as gender, body image, religious beliefs, amongst others, the system provides a kind of measure of implicit biases in that direction. This, as expected, raised many concerns in that the use of big data and statistical results was probably too much of a stretch to detect something as profound and as serious as a bias, but also whether the real response time was associated with each person's own beliefs or those pervading in society and that need to be overcome when making conscious decisions about associations. Does a higher IAT score truly indicate that an individual will behave in a more biased manner, or does it merely reflect broad cultural associations?

Undeniably, this serves as a compelling illustration of the grave ethical consequences inherent in using big data for drawing conclusions, particularly when combined with statistical outcomes. There isn't a definitive answer to these concerns yet, which underscores the importance of educating students on this topic. They need to comprehend how these statistical investigations and inferred extrapolations often capture media attention, despite their potentially misleading nature.

## *Advanced robots and humanoids.*

Beyond chatbots there are humanoids. These anthropomorphic robots utilize the advanced capabilities of chatbots in the shape of a humanoid that can interact with users in a seamless way.

There have been many demonstrations of prototypes that can do this, including several high-profile appearances on the Jimmy Fallon show. As of yet, there aren't still any mainstream applications of the new advances in AI and natural language processing to humanoids, but these are sure to come very soon and we can expect to have very advanced prototypes that will eventually make it to the market. These humanoids will surely replicate the characteristics of ChatGPT into fully fledged integrated robots that resemble humans, and pose some unique and unprecedented challenges.

It is, once more, for us educators to try to discern what our reactions will be and how to make sense of these humanlike companions that are soon to invade our lives.

These almost preternatural creations can elicit all kinds of responses, since any close resemblance to our own sense of humanity can trigger off some quite unique reactions. The Uncanny Valley theory, proposed by robotics professor Masahiro Mori, suggests that as a robot or digital representation becomes more human-like, our emotional response towards it becomes increasingly positive until it reaches a point of near-human likeness, where the response suddenly turns to strong revulsion. This dramatic dip in emotional response is the "uncanny valley", reflecting a discomfort with things that seem almost, but not exactly, human.

We can relate to this theory when we see freaky looking contraptions that, for the time being, are not attractive or easy to relate with, but which may become even indistinguishable from humans in the not too distant future.

The field of Roboethics is already studying interactions between robots and humans and some of the implications related to advanced robots simulating consciousness and even feelings. The same experience that we are now facing when interacting with chatbots like ChatGPT, who have almost human-like abilities to converse and relate to us in the impersonal aseptic environment of the keyboard and the screen, will be exponentially magnified when interacting almost naturally with a human-looking contraption. As usual, there are no direct answers to the question of how this will impact our lives, but understanding how these robots work, their limitations, and why they seem to have superhuman capabilities in some respect is undoubtedly useful for students to be better prepared for a world that has become increasingly unpredictable.

## The Most Human Human.

At the end of the day, it is about guiding our students into redefining their sense of humanity in the age of AI. As artificial intelligence applications become more and more prevalent and transparent and ubiquitous, we always need to be reminded of what makes us human and how to nurture and maintain our sense of humanity from a very early age.

Brian Christian[6] is an author and IT expert who once acted as the chatbot counterpart in an AI contest that used to be held in the UK, the Loebner Prize, which pitted against each other the most advanced chatbot software at the time.

The contest took place in the following form: for several

rounds, human judges had to engage in text based chats, not knowing whether at the other end of the screen there was an AI-powered chatbot system, or another human who conversed with the judges in the same way. At the end of each round the judges had to discern whether they had spoken to a computer or to a human. The AI chatbots which were able to more successfully fool the judges into making them believe that it was a human, was the one that scored more points, and ultimately obtained the Loebner Prize.

The contest included not only a prize for the most intelligent computer system, even though none of them until ChatGPT were able to fully pass what is known as the Turing test, the ability for these chatbots to pass as humans, but also to "The Most Human Human", a coveted prize for that person that most successfully was able to let the judges at the other end of the screen know that they were human.

The author relates his experience in being one of the human counterparts that conversed with the judges and how he prepared for the contest trying to convey his humanity in ways that were unequivocal so that the judges at the other end of the screen could know that he was indeed a human and not a machine. In the process, he was forced to reflect and understand how he could convey his humanity through the detached medium of the conversation screen.

This is a great exercise for students, to pretend that they themselves are at the other end of a chat with another person who knows nothing about them. How would they interact with the other person so that they can prove that they are humans? How could they, for example, at this age and time, distinguish themselves from an AI when chatting on WhatsApp or any of the other instant messaging applications? We already know the drill. There are no right or wrong answers, but rather the exercise of reflecting and providing some critical feedback on some of these developments and how they may affect our students' lives, not just in the future, but right now.

## What we need to do in schools.

Finally, the question that begs is asking is, faced with all these overwhelming stimuli and emerging set of ever increasing complexities, what should we educators do at schools?

To start with, take advantage of any opportunities we might have to discuss and reflect on these issues and present these dilemmas to students, not to find a correct or right answer, but for them to become more aware of some of these, in many cases, implicit implications of the development of AI and other advanced technological developments.

It is also our role to provide a doses of human moderation and a more humane perspective on these topics, understanding that as advanced as these capabilities may be, it is paramount for us to be able to guide our students into nurturing and nourishing ever more their human presence, connecting with their emotions, their sense of self, and being aware of what it takes to be human.

Needless to say, there is no one answer for this, but the very exercise of engaging in these reflections and discussions is valuable intrinsically, as many of the process that we are engaged in in education at this point.

## Summary:

*AI and Everyday Life*

- AI is becoming deeply integrated into daily life, affecting education and social interactions.
- The rise of AI brings about ethical and societal implications that educators must understand and address.

### AI and Other Advanced Technologies

- AI, big data, augmented reality, and advanced robots pose unique challenges to students growing up in a rapidly evolving world.
- Understanding how these technologies work is vital for students to anticipate their impacts and become critical users.

### Big Data in Education

- Big data involves collecting, storing, and analyzing large amounts of information, and its use in education is growing.
- Several ethical concerns arise from using big data in education.

### Ethical Concerns Related to Big Data

- Privacy and Data Protection: There's a risk of data misuse and breaches.
- Consent: Students or guardians need to clearly understand data collection and usage.
- Equity: There's a risk that predictive algorithms could worsen inequalities.
- Transparency: Algorithms' complexity could lead to a lack of clarity in decision-making.
- Data Ownership: There are questions about who owns the data collected.
- Use of Predictive Analytics: There are ethical issues if these are used to track students or determine their potential.

*AI-Based Adaptive Systems and Transparency*

- AI-based systems for personalized learning can be beneficial, but they also raise issues related to transparency.
- Users might have the right to understand decisions made by algorithms, particularly in the education sector.

*Implicit Decisions by AI Systems*

- AI systems make decisions for users, such as in self-driving cars and other applications embedded with AI.
- The MIT Moral Machine highlights ethical dilemmas linked to AI decision-making.

*Understanding Human-Designed Decisions in AI*

- It's important to understand that human-designed decisions are embedded in AI software, emphasizing the need for comprehension of these systems.

*Augmented Reality and Smart Glasses*

- Smart glasses can interpret surroundings, identify objects, and provide contextual information based on algorithms.
- Ethical issues arise when this technology is applied to people, potentially recognizing and gathering information on individuals in real-time.
- There are concerns about how such technology could affect spontaneous human interactions and personal privacy.

*Social Networks and Privacy Concerns*

- Teachers and educators play a crucial role in guiding young users about privacy concerns related to social networks.
- Users need to understand the trade-offs involved in using free applications, including the potential exposure of their personal data for commercial purposes.
- Understanding these privacy issues and how data is used is essential for users to make informed decisions.

*The Implicit Bias Problem*

- Harvard's Project Implicit used big data to measure implicit biases. This raised questions about the validity of using statistical results to detect biases and the influence of societal beliefs on these biases.
- The use of big data for such purposes has ethical implications and emphasizes the need for education on the topic.

*Advanced Robots and Humanoids*

- Humanoid robots incorporating advanced AI and natural language processing may soon become mainstream.
- The Uncanny Valley theory suggests that near-human likeness in robots can trigger a strong negative emotional response.
- The emerging field of Roboethics is studying interactions between robots and humans and the implications of advanced robots simulating consciousness.

*The Most Human Human*

- The Loebner Prize, an AI contest, included a prize for "the most human human" - the person who could most convincingly prove they were human and not an AI.
- This contest encourages reflection on what it means to be human and how to convey humanity in the digital age.

*What We Need to Do in Schools*

- Educators should facilitate discussions on these issues to increase students' awareness of the implications of AI and other advanced technologies.
- The goal is to guide students towards a humane perspective, nurturing their emotional self-awareness and understanding of what it means to be human.

*Prompts and activities*

- Give real-life examples of algorithmic decisions that affect the general public.
- Provide real-life examples of applications of AI that are commonplace and that are mostly transparent to the general user.
- Explain in detail how algorithms for self-driving cars are designed. How does it pre-resolve, for example, any alternatives between hitting passersby or endangering the occupants of the car?
- Give examples of other instances in which there might be decisions premade by algorithms and that could affect humans.
- Give examples of ethical dilemmas associated with the use of AI.

- Explain how pattern recognition works and how smartglasses utilize this technology to identify objects and places.
- Discuss how smart glasses can recognize a person and how it could eventually provide the user of the smart glasses with contextual information about the person, describing in detail the inner workings of an algorithm that provides information on the person after it recognizes the face.
- Discuss ethical concerns stemming from the use of smart glasses.
- Provide a summary of what personal information social networks gather about users. (Detailed information can be obtained about a specific social network.)
- Do our devices listen to us? Explain how, on occasions, after having a conversation an advertisement related to a topic in that conversation pops up in our devices.
- Summarize how users can take control of their privacy through their social network accounts.
- Simulate an example of big data information obtained in the context of a school where administrators would have to make decisions that pose an ethical dilemma.
- Provide examples of how big data is collected in the education context and how it can inform decisions made by administrators and educators.
- Explain the theory of the Uncanny Valley and how that might affect our relationship with humanoids.
- Give examples of applications of Roboethics to real life situations.
- Explain, in simple terms, and in detail, how

> humanoids work, highlighting the various sensors and how it responds to human interactions.

## Activity

<u>Designing a Context-Aware Facial Recognition Augmented Reality Algorithm: Exploring Ethical Implications</u>

<u>Lesson Objective:</u> Students will engage in critical thinking and discussions about the ethical implications of facial recognition augmented reality algorithms by designing a context-aware system and exploring various scenarios involving the use of such technology.

<u>Grade Level</u>: As presented, this activity would be most appropriate for students at High School level, but it can be adapted for Middle School and even Elementary School students by toning down some of the questions.

<u>Lesson Outline:</u>
    I.    Introduction
- A. Briefly introduce the concept of facial recognition and augmented reality technology.
- B. Explain the objective of the lesson, emphasizing the focus on ethical implications and contextual information.

    II.    Group Discussion
- A. Divide students into small groups (3-4 students per group).
- B. Instruct each group to discuss the potential benefits and drawbacks of facial recognition augmented reality algorithms.
- C. Have each group report back to the class,

summarizing their discussion points.

### III. Design Activity

Students are supervising the final deployment of a context aware facial recognition augmented reality software, that would enable a real-time hardware device, such as glasses, to recognize a person and provide contextual information to the user. Their role is to work with the programmers to develop the software, its features and applications.

Discussion Questions:

1. What contextual information should the system provide about the recognized person?
2. What privacy and consent concerns should be addressed?
3. How can the system minimize potential biases and discrimination?
4. What safeguards can be implemented to prevent misuse of the technology?

### IV. Reflection Questions

A. Have each group present their algorithm design to the class.

B. Consider the following reflection questions:

1. Do you agree with the contextual information provided in the algorithm designs? Why or why not?
2. How do you feel about the potential invasion of privacy associated with facial recognition technology? Should people have the right to opt out of the system and be "non-recognizable"?
3. How can we balance the benefits of this technology with its potential negative consequences?
4. What role should government and policymakers play in regulating the use of facial recognition and augmented reality technology?

The ultimate goal is for students to become more aware of

some of the underlying implications of advanced systems and how companies are making important ethical decisions behind the scenes.

# THE FUTURE OF SCHOOLS - REDEFINED

The advent of ChatGPT and other generative AI applications is, without a doubt, one of the most significant and surprising technological changes in history. Like never before, since other momentous changes had been a little bit more gradual in their development and application, a technological change has had such a massive and rapid impact on our lives, as well as harboring a potential for unlimited development that is truly unfathomable.

As we will analyze subsequently, there is a real risk of loss of jobs and other societal changes, but the real revolution, one that may even threaten the existence of schools, is in education. Many questions have sprung in the little time that ChatGPT has been available to the general public: will it replace teachers, will it, if not, change the role of teachers to an extent that it is unrecognizable as we know it now, are schools actually going to be rendered obsolete?

Only time will tell. As with other technological applications, education has a recalcitrant way of remaining immune to even the most drastic changes, although this time even the seemingly immutable traditional school model is really at risk.

Inasmuch as these questions may generate tremendous

uncertainty, we are no position to answer them now, but what we can do is try to break down potential developments, risks, and implications to attempt to shape up rather than predict the future.

## Generative AI applications - what they can do as related to schools and education

In a nutshell, ChatGPT is an omniscient database that can retrieve knowledge in any shape or form as we know it. This is, ultimately, the utopian objective of schools as we know them: to help students learn as much as possible and to be able to express that knowledge in various ways and forms.

So the initial premise is that ChatGPT and the family of related generative AI applications is the perfect final product; that is, it has all the capabilities that are required of students in any school anywhere in the world.

The implications, give or take, are obvious and direct. ChatGPT can be used to complete any school assignment whatsoever, in the way that most schools are structured and assessments administered.

And here comes the first serious risk, one that needs to be addressed immediately, since, regardless of what a school may decide, students will have access at home to ChatGPT. The structure of schooling is predicated, and even as we know how much traditional school needs to change, this principle still holds true, in the progressive acquisition of knowledge and cognitive skills following children's and teenagers' development as they grow up. Once more, even though they are hopelessly outdated, school curriculums all over the world are designed with what is a time proven sequence of increasingly more difficult and complex set of skills that students acquire, within a learning process that involves learning and exercising those cognitive skills until they master them.

The usual process involves, with varying degrees of difficulty, depending on the student and the area or subject in question, learning a concept or skill, increasing the depth and complexity involved, exercising and finally acquiring those skills by demonstrating proficiency in them. With all their limitations, assessments are intended to gauge whether students have acquired the skills and the knowledge that are considered to be important for their learning and which will serve them well in their current and future lives.

Now there is a tool, infinitely available and customizable, that can, at best, have them master those skills, and, at worst, do things for them, bypassing the full extent of the learning experience. The temptation is probably too powerful to override, when faced with a certain difficulty in comprehension, not knowing how to fully answer a problem or exercise, or any other instance in which students are confronted with any steepness in the learning curve, having these ubiquitous and omnipresent assistants that can explain or do for us is probably too much to resist.

This means that, at every step in the full extent of the formative stage of students´ school experience, there is a real risk that some of those cognitive skills will be stifled and mastery masked by the intervention, explicit or implicit, of generative AI applications.

How can school address this? There are probably no good answers for this question, and despite what could be our best efforts of becoming increasingly creative in assessments, it would be very hard to develop evaluation instruments that are invulnerable to generative AI.

## The AI immunized school

This brings us to our next section, probably the most important in this book, related to how we can attempt to develop a new model of schooling that, if not immune, at least develops some healthy antibodies to the pervasive and unstoppable influence of ChatGPT and other generative AI applications.

## Reinforcing All Things Metacognitive

At a time when cognition is superseded by AI and even the Internet, as we knew all along, schools needed to vastly reinforce emphasis on metacognition, which is just a fancy name that we like to use for anything that relates to learning how to learn, and making students more aware of their learning.

Now it is not just cognition that is at risk, the ability of ChatGPT and the other applications to best our students - and even many adult experts - of the full range of skills that are required in schools, it is more important than ever to render all aspects of the learning process as visible as possible.

This means - lo and behold - that whenever we ask students to do any school related tasks, as we always should, but now forced by the circumstance that there is this unspeakable monster that can do things for them, we should explain and justify why a certain skill needs to be acquired and should not be offloaded to ChatGPT.

If we request that our students do not outsource their assignment to generative AI, we must explain, in as much detail as possible, why it is important that they do so and not rely on the venerable AI tool.

Problem solving, summarizing, extracting main ideas from a text, thinking out a problem, breaking it out in its component parts, and any other school assignment the can now be easily handled by ChatGPT needs to be justified to students for them to be aware of the importance of learning the skills themselves and not handing them over to the AI.

Subsequently, and, again, we are finally obligated to do as we should always have done, the subject matter itself cedes preeminence to the skill, and when evaluating students what we need to know is not whether they remember content or if they have apprehended certain facts but rather whether they have learned the relevant skills.

So, once more, one of the main antidotes to ChatGPT is explicitly highlighting and emphasizing the metacognitive aspects of learning, so that students can gain greater awareness about their learning process. As new skills emerge (writing prompts!) It is essential that learners become more self-aware of all aspects of the learning process so that they themselves might want to refrain from an indiscriminate use of ChatGPT and can make informed decisions as to where and when to use it.

## Project Based Learning

As it could be expected by now, the norm seems to be that all the practices that were considered progressive and beneficial to overcome the traditional model of school are also the ones that are proving to be increasingly immune to the generative AI invasion.

Project-based learning, design, working in groups, collaborating, developing products, and any creative expression that involves working with peers, successively improving assignments, learning from mistakes, and doing on-the-fly research is not only the right thing to do, but in this case, a great way to become less dependent on ChatGPT. ChatGPT provides a shortcut to results, the ley, as we knew all along, is to focus on and assess the process.

For some of the intermediate stages, like doing research or even developing rubrics to analyze projects, generative AI tools may prove to be invaluable resources that take care of some of the more mechanical and repetitive tasks involved in the process. And, once more, it is up to us teachers to try to enhance the metacognitive or higher order thinking skills that are involved in the process.

It can be argued that the individual tasks that make up the project development process may be outsourced to ChatGPT, but, in any case, it is also the nature of the teacher involvement in the process to be continuously supervising and receiving feedback from the groups. It is that part of the process which allows educators to better monitor what is being done by the students themselves and what can eventually be plugged into the generative AI.

## Assessment

Assessment has been the variable bête noir when it came to educational reform, since, despite the best-intentioned efforts to bring forth a new outlook on how to evaluate students, by far and large, the dominant species in schools still remains the sit-down written test, closed book, no retest.

ChatGPT and a related family of generative AI applications, with their stated capability of doing absolutely everything that can be asked of a student in the school context, have challenged educators to rethink their assessments by several orders of magnitude. However, and this is a big difference with respect to the previous pre-ChatGPT scenario, it is now almost an impossible challenge.

In effect, Generative AI can perform the whole range of tasks that are demanded of students in the school context, even by the most stringent standards as posed by external exams, advanced placement or international examinations. It is a tall order, even for the most innovative teachers, to devise assessments that can be immune to being outsourced to ChatGPT or other AI applications.

As with many other aspects of schooling, assessment will perforce have to become what it should have been long ago, an interactive personal process of frequent feedback from the teacher. The only way to immunize assessments from ChatGPT is for the teacher to have frequent back-and-forth interactions with either the individual student or the group developing a project, fostering discussions and providing suggestions. All in all, it is, no surprise here, what we have always known we should do, that is, engage in formative assessment in as great a detail as possible.

This is to say that it is not so much in the nature of the assessment, which, again, is almost impossible to make it ChatGPT-proof, but rather in the assessment process itself that lies the key to successfully navigating these uncertain times. Needless to say, any assignment that involves creative input from the students themselves, a genuine personal expression in the process of demonstrating their knowledge, stands a better chance of not being AI generated.

As its use has demonstrated even in this short time, however, ChatGPT is very good at providing creative answers and solutions, mimicking the creative process to an extent that can be considered uncanny. It is always laudable to try to infuse creative assignments into assessments, but even those, if not properly followed up, can be generated by these new AI tools.

## Cheating, academic integrity and learning

Any discussion of ChatGPT and its use in education would be woefully incomplete if we do not name the elephant in the room, that is, the issue of cheating, academic integrity, and students using ChatGPT and the other generative AI tools to do their assignments and get, of course, higher marks in the process.

It needs to be stated, so as to clear the air, that none of the tools, including the OpenAI Text Classifier (https://platform.openai.com/ai-text-classifier), can detect, despite what they claim to do, whether a text is generated by AI or not. Because of the statistical nature of the process, in which generative AI systems predict what the next token is and translate it into words, no two answers to the same question are going to be alike, and the ability to produce humanlike text that these applications have demonstrated renders them undetectable to even the most advanced plagiarism checker.

In any case, and this can be easily checked, merely infusing a couple of errors within even a long text can shift it from "broadly written by an AI" to "entirely written by a human". So let's accept the premise that teachers will not have at their disposal any tool that will allow them to automatically detect whether a text has been produced by an AI or not.

The so-called issue of academic integrity has been at the forefront of the concerns expressed by educators, administrators and policymakers regarding the use of ChatGPT for school. International examination boards, like the International Baccalaureate, have even explicitly stated that anything generated by ChatGPT needs to be cited and acknowledged in any work produced by students as part of coursework.

The fact that the issue of whether students are going to use generative AI to cheat is the dominant theme in discussions regarding its application to education speaks volumes in itself. One of the many problems with traditional education, and one which is, undoubtedly, at the center of many of the problems we still face, is that education has become more centered on assessment than learning. Even at the risk of sounding idealistic or philosophical, we need to understand that assessment is about gauging student progress in learning, and not the main objective of the learning process per se. We have glorified assessment to the point that, in the narrative of schools, it supersedes learning.

The question we should be asking ourselves is not whether students are cutting corners by using generative AI to fake their assignments, but what the impact of these tools is on learning.

Sure, we can redesign our assessments and instill any

measures to preserve the sacrosanct "integrity" associated with the academic process, but that is missing the main point. As we should have done long before ChatGPT appeared, we need to redefine the focus of school to make it more student centered and more learning centered, understanding that assessment is, at best, just a way to measure learning progress.

What if we had no more grades in school? What if assessment was 100% formative, based on rubrics that were narrative and not quantifiable? Would that make school impossible? Would teachers not be able to fulfill their roles and inspire students to become lifelong learners?

There is no expected answer to these rhetorical questions but, if anything, the advent of generative AI may serve as a powerful catalyst to refocus our efforts, our energy, and our reaction to this major disruptive force in education on what really matters, students and their learning.

## The double standard

An excessively paternalistic view on the use of ChatGPT that is mostly focused on preventing cheating can also result in a dangerous double standard that confronts us with an ethical dilemma. Many teachers are rejoicing at ChatGPT's almost magical ability to produce some of the most dreaded administrative instruments that teachers are confronted with on a daily basis.

Lesson plans, evaluations, rubrics, reports, most of the less enlightening tasks associated with teaching are being offloaded to generative AI, with no discernible effects, much rather with some self-evident benefits in terms of the quality, detail, and even knowledge base involved in their creation. Administrators would not dare question whether a lesson plan, activity, assessment instrument or rubric has been created by an AI or done by the teacher from scratch, especially if they are not taken verbatim, but modified and edited by teachers themselves. This may create a dangerous double standard: what is acceptable for teachers and why is it that they can use the tool freely at will and students can't?

It may be argued - more on this later - that because teachers are experts at what they do and can discern what is mechanical from what is truly a professional expression of their expertise, it is acceptable for them to use AI tools for the sake of efficiency and even quality of work. Being expert professionals grants teachers the possibility of reviewing what is produced by the AI, evaluating whether it is accurate and factually correct, and even improve it so that a better in product is generated, always for the benefit of the students who are the recipients of teacher's travails.

If we accept this premise, that teachers may have a proverbial license to use the AI based on their having gone already significantly further down the learning road then students have, it is an implicit, but very significant, acknowledgment of the validity of ChatGPT and these other AI apps to assist and enhance the productive process in the field of learning.

The implications are, as we will see in the succeeding section, that it may very well be that the objective of schooling is to develop the skills necessary to operate generative AI applications at the highest possible level.

## *Pen and paper? Please no!*

The worst thing we can do is revert to pen and paper. Yes, the archaic procedure for students to complete assignments or evaluations is blissfully free of ChatGPT and many other technology mediated interferences, but it makes absolutely no sense to go back to the dark ages.

It is almost nonsensical to try to justify why schools should not go back to pen and paper as a way to counteract ChatGPT. The world is rapidly digitizing and the skills students need to succeed in the 21st century are increasingly related to digital literacy. In this environment, pen and paper cannot keep up with the efficiency, speed, and multifunctionality provided by digital tools. As we all know, digital documents are easy to edit, share, and store, which is especially critical in a collaborative learning environment.

Furthermore, digital tools provide an array of features like spell-check, grammar suggestions, instant translations, and accessibility options which are not possible with traditional pen and paper. By insisting on pen and paper, we limit students' ability to develop the digital skills they will inevitably need in their future careers.

## *Social emotional learning, contact with nature, physical activity.*

The issue of how now we need to make true on what we knew all along is a recurring theme in this chapter. But it is an inescapable reality. Schools should long ago have embraced a transformation to shift the main focus of schooling from factual recall, rote learning and a preponderance on contents rather than skills to other more important developmental activities that target a more holistic, well-rounded approach to education.

And it so happens, in what is, again, another leitmotif of our discussions, that it is precisely those activities that are not only "protected" from ChatGPT but also can benefit immensely from its use.

It may very well be that the school of the future is not just high-tech, but mostly defined by a preponderance of activities that are related to learning to be in nature, physical activity and team sports, social emotional learning, connecting with our emotions, contemplative practices, arts and crafts, and other areas in the curriculum that are currently considered marginal and either left to extracurricular activities or relegated in terms of their time assignment in the school schedule.

A very important point must be made here: because the nature of these activities involves interacting with the real-life environment, be it another person, nature, or playing a team sport, the use of generative AI to inform those interactions is undoubtedly beneficial and enriching, thus paving the way for what could be the ultimate application of these tools for learning.

When education authentically intersects with real-life contexts - as it ideally should - the use of generative AI and the resulting efficiency in the learning process can enhance our knowledge acquisition. This, in turn, bolsters our interactions within various contexts, whether it's interpersonal communication, participation in team sports, or the exploration of nature.

From a pedagogical point of view, if we find a way to eventually reconcile ourselves with the abbreviated learning process that is explicit in the use of ChatGPT, it will allow us to apply that knowledge, once more, in a real-life context unlearn experientially from those interactions, in what we know have always been considered more meaningful, memorable, and genuine learning experiences.

## *Reassessing cognitive skills*

One of the main consequences of the generalized potential future use of ChatGPT and the generative AI is a redefinition of what, until now, have been considered core, essential cognitive skills.

Only a few months ago, for example, what was known as the field of abstractive summarization, the ability to use AI software to summarize texts by rewriting them and preserving their meaning in an abridged version, was in the rarefied reality of experimental prototypes developed by university researchers and not yet available to the general public. In a fell swoop, ChatGPT has obliterated those efforts and placed that capacity, of summarizing, synthesizing, extracting main points and ideas and any other simplification of text, just a few keystrokes away from mainstream users.

As anybody who has been school is aware, reading comprehension in all its shapes, forms and flavors, has been, justifiably, one of the premium cognitive skills to be acquired by students when they complete their formal schooling. This was rooted in the necessity to read large volumes of text in order to gain knowledge from them, extract the main concepts and ideas, and understand them, as the main medium for transmitting knowledge.

Now, and in the future, in theory, there is no need for us to read any long text or bulk, since ChatGPT and its cousins can do that for us with utmost and impeccable efficiency - this is one of the applications that are almost error-free. Reading a long text or bulk, however, is not just about utilitarian learning. As neuroscience has shown, the brain needs a slower rhythm to learn some concepts and ideas, and there is, of course, the rich background, context, and expressive possibilities that are offered by books and long texts.

On the other hand, and this is about the historical main victim of education, opportunity cost, the time spent in reading and deriving learning and understanding from a long text could be invested in either learning more or applying that knowledge in the real-life context. Generative AI can, indeed, be a very powerful tool both to increase the volume of learning as well as the speed with which it is done.

## What about writing?

The other quintessential related skill for schooling, writing, is also at question. Generative AI can produce text of any length, depth, complexity, literary form, completely customized to our most detailed specifications. It may be argued that is no longer necessary to know the right answer, but rather to generate detailed prompts and fine-tune what generative AI produces in order to act more as a human editors than writers.

But how do we get there? This is probably the key question related to the application of generative AI to education. We appreciate that anybody who has higher order skills can make a truly fantastic slave of ChatGPT and vastly improve their quality and level of output in whatever field they are dealing with.

The question that has no answer is to how we actually get to the point where we can assess, engineer detailed prompts and improve writing output from a generative AI so that it produces the desired text. And, even though we will not know until there has been a more sustained use of these tools, it is, in all likelihood, by writing ourselves that we will get to the point, as many of us have, where we can take full advantage of generative AI to write better than we ourselves could do.

## From cognitive to metacognitive skills

This dilemma, fundamental and at the heart of any positive possible implementation of generative AI tools, can only be resolved with the now familiar shift from cognitive to meta cognitive skills in school. The fundamental shift needed, as exemplified with reading and writing, and that can be applied to all of the other disciplines, is that we need to learn and practice skills ourselves in order to be, eventually, in a position to outsource them to a generative AI.

But, and as we have seen repeatedly, at the heart of this transformation lies a focus on the skills themselves, on making students more aware of learning to learn, what is commonly referred to as metacognitive skills. At this stage, it seems to be that the end goal would be to become super users of generative AI so that we can get the best of both worlds, our human expression, creativity and intelligence coupled with the vast knowledge base, inexhaustible and instantaneous capacity for generation of these applications.

Even as we acknowledge that the objective of schooling may have shifted, and without the benefit of hindsight, it seems fairly obvious that the only way to acquire the higher order skills required to fully exploit to the capacities of generative AI is to go through skills ourselves, and to engage in a thoughtful and intentional learning process that explicitly prioritizes the acquisition of such skills.

This requires a much-needed shift in mindset regarding what is important at schools, and what we assess in our students, whilst not totally disregarding contents. This is not too different from what school reform should have been in the age of the Internet, but the new scenario with intelligent agents that can do everything for us is infinitely more forceful in the need for change.

## Summary

*The Future of Schools - Redefined*

- AI applications like ChatGPT may drastically alter the function and structure of schools.
- The significant potential impact of AI on education could necessitate a complete overhaul of current systems.

*Implications of Generative AI for Education*

- Generative AI could perform academic tasks, possibly overshadowing students' personal learning journeys.
- There's a risk of inhibiting cognitive skill development as students may become overly reliant on AI.

*Addressing the Risks Posed by Generative AI in Schools*

- Designing AI-proof assessments could pose significant challenges.
- Constructing a new educational paradigm that can withstand the effects of generative AI could be crucial.

*Reinforcing Metacognition in Schools*

- AI's emergence necessitates a stronger emphasis on metacognition, or understanding one's own learning process.
- Teachers need to underscore the significance of students learning certain skills firsthand, instead of delegating tasks to AI.

*The Role of Project-Based Learning*

- Project-based learning might be a solution to mitigate overreliance on AI tools.
- AI could be beneficial for managing routine tasks, allowing educators to concentrate on fostering students' higher-order cognitive skills.

*Challenges and Opportunities in Assessment*

- Generative AI compels educators to redesign assessments to be more imaginative and engaging.
- Regular formative feedback could ensure students are genuinely doing their work, not AI.

*Cheating, Academic Integrity, and Learning*

- AI presents potential issues with academic honesty, as students might use it to complete assignments.
- There's a need for AI-detection tools and strategies to maintain academic integrity.

Refocusing on Learning Rather Than Assessment

- AI's advent calls for a shift from concentrating on evaluations to focusing on actual learning.
- Implementing radical changes such as eliminating grading in favor of narrative evaluations might prove advantageous.

*The Double Standard in AI Usage*

- There are serious ethical debates around the educational use of AI, such as ChatGPT.
- An imbalance exists where teachers can use AI for tasks, but students are prohibited.

*Teacher's Expertise and AI*

- Teachers can effectively use AI due to their professional knowledge.
- Teachers' content understanding enables them to revise AI-generated outputs, affirming the usefulness of tools like ChatGPT.

*The Risks of Reverting to Pen and Paper*

- Returning to traditional pen and paper assignments to avoid AI usage is a regressive move.
- Modern digital tools, necessary for today's world, offer advantages that traditional methods can't match.

*Prioritizing Holistic Development in Education*

- A shift from rote learning to comprehensive educational experiences is required.
- Generative AI has potential applications that can enhance realistic learning experiences.

*Reassessing Cognitive Skills in Light of AI*

- Generative AI might change our understanding of fundamental cognitive skills.
- AI's capacity to summarize and synthesize large volumes of text might diminish the importance of traditional reading comprehension.

*Impact on Writing Skills*

- Generative AI can create intricate text, reducing the need for traditional writing skills.
- The emphasis is on learning how to guide and refine AI-generated text.

*Transition from Cognitive to Metacognitive Skills*

- The shift from cognitive to metacognitive skills is crucial for successfully integrating AI tools.
- A shift in focus in schools towards higher-order skills acquisition, rather than memorizing content, is called for.

# AI TO THE TEST: A CASE STUDY

As a final exercise to gauge how effective generative AI systems can be to assist the learning in a concrete project, we will be posting a hypothetical challenge in breaking down in both scenarios, pre-and post ChatGPT. The hope is that by doing so, we will be able to discern and compare both approaches to learning, not with the goal of comparing which one is better but rather to understand how we can optimize learning.

**The problem:** In this interdisciplinary science project, students are challenged to design a bio regenerative recycling system for a cabin in the woods that is off the grid. The objective is for students to learn about the processes engaged in recycling and regeneration, go through multiple stages of design and apply their creativity through this interdisciplinary science project.

No initial parameters are given, but the owner of the cabin is ready to supply students with whatever information they require in order to design the most adequate system.

For the sake of our study, we will suppose that students have a mid-level high school science background, and have heard of but never actually studied bio regenerative recycling systems.

## *Pre-AI world*

Solving the problem and producing a concrete design for the recycling system would require:

- An initial analysis whereby students, individually or in teams, break down the problem at hand and plan to solve it. Even if they can't initially lay out a full plan for learning about the topic at hand and designing the system, they will, at least, have a preliminary discussion on where to start from.
- General research on bio regenerative recycling systems, types, real-life implementation, examples of use.
- From there, probably break down the components of the system into subsystems, and further research the various available solutions and technologies for the problem at hand.
- Subsequently, we would be faced with the problem of how to best match the solutions that we have researched up with the real needs of this cabin.
- This would require a fair amount of analysis in terms of what to ask the cabin owner in terms of input for the system.
- Once that information is obtained, for each of the components of the system, it would be necessary to understand the range of operation, how much each of them can process, and to choose one particular solution to adopt for the system.
- The system would then need to be put together, in some kind of diagram or conceptual layout.
- An important issue remains in the design of the system, related to how these systems interact with each other and how to simulate a flow to see if they can process the inputs they receive. This is quite a complex endeavor, requiring for the designers to develop some kind of algorithm that receives a daily dose of inputs and estimates outputs for the

system.
- Research daily input and output in terms of the number of occupants of the cabin.
- Run some kind of simulation through a spreadsheet or ad hoc algorithm to see if the system works.
- Make any tweaks or redesigns that might prove necessary.

As we can infer from the sequence of steps outlined, this is quite a tough problem, and one that would need substantial help from the part of the teacher and/or an expert, as well as possibly some simplifications related to the actual testing of the system.

The whole process can take a number of lessons and is probably a multiweek project.

### *Using generative AI*

We will now attempt to run the same process with the help of ChatGPT.

This would be a possible initial prompt:

- We need to design a bio regenerative recycling system for a cabin that is off the grid. How do these systems work and what components do they usually have?

Here is ChatGPT's answer:

> A bio-regenerative recycling system is a comprehensive way to manage resources and waste that mimics natural ecosystems, which can be especially valuable for an off-grid cabin. These systems are typically self-sustaining and designed to reduce waste, maximize efficiency, and take full advantage of renewable resources.
> 
> Here are the major components and processes you might

consider:

1. Water Recycling System: This is key to ensuring a reliable supply of clean water. The system typically includes rainwater harvesting, greywater recycling, and a composting toilet.

   - Rainwater Harvesting: Collect rainwater from roof run-off and store it in a cistern. Filter and treat it for various uses like washing and even drinking if properly treated.

   - Greywater Recycling: Greywater is wastewater from sources like the shower, bathroom sinks, and washing machine. This can be treated and reused for toilet flushing, watering plants, and other non-potable uses.

   - Composting Toilet: This eliminates the need for a septic system and reduces water usage. The composting process breaks down human waste into a safe, nutrient-rich compost that can be used to enrich soil.

2. Food Production: This might include a small-scale indoor or outdoor garden or even an aquaponics system. With proper planning, you can grow a surprising amount of food in a small space.

   - Aquaponics: This is a combination of aquaculture (raising fish) and hydroponics (growing plants in water without soil). The waste from the fish serves as organic food for the plants, and the plants naturally filter the water for the fish.

3. Energy Generation and Management: Off-grid living requires alternative energy sources. Solar power is most common, but wind or hydro power

can also be viable options depending on the location of the cabin. Additionally, energy storage (e.g., batteries) and efficient use of energy (e.g., LED lights, energy-efficient appliances) are essential.

4. Waste Management and Resource Recovery: Anything that can't be reused directly can often be composted or used in some other way. This could include composting organic kitchen waste or even using a small-scale bio-digester to convert waste into biogas for cooking and heating.

5. Air Management System: This might include ventilation for maintaining air quality, as well as plants to naturally improve air quality and provide a bit of extra oxygen.

6. Education/Information System: This would be some way of tracking and managing the various systems, perhaps including sensors to monitor water and energy use, the health of the garden/aquaponics system, etc. This could also include education on how to maintain and troubleshoot the systems.

By integrating all these components, you can create a closed-loop system that mimics the cycles of nature. This can provide a sustainable way to meet many of the basic needs of the cabin's inhabitants, with minimal reliance on outside resources or infrastructure.

- Students, as per the teachers objectives, may then want to delve deeper into some of the science processes involved in each of the stages identified in the answer. Let's suppose that we continue down the path towards the eventual design of the system itself.

**Prompt:** What input data do we need in order to design the system? What should we ask of the cabin owner about the cabin to be able to solve the problem?

**Answer:**

> In order to design a bio-regenerative recycling system for an off-grid cabin, you'll need quite a bit of information. Here are the key pieces of data you should gather:
>
> 1. Location and Climate: You'll need to know where the cabin is located and what the local climate is like. This will help determine what types of renewable energy are viable, how much rainwater you can expect to collect, what types of plants can be grown, etc.
> 2. Size of the Cabin and Available Land: The size of the cabin will dictate how much space is available for systems like greywater recycling or aquaponics within the structure itself. The amount of available land can also impact your options for outdoor systems like composting toilets or vegetable gardens.
> 3. Number of Occupants and Lifestyle: The number of people using the cabin and their lifestyles will affect the design. For example, the amount of water and energy needed will depend on how many people are living in the cabin and what their daily habits are.
> 4. Budget: The cabin owner's budget will obviously play a big role in determining what systems are feasible.

> 5. Purpose of the Cabin: Is this a full-time residence, a vacation home, a rental property, etc.? This will affect how the systems are used and what the maintenance requirements will be.
> 6. Local Laws and Regulations: You'll need to know what's legally allowed in terms of things like rainwater collection, waste disposal, etc.
> 7. Existing Infrastructure: Does the cabin already have some form of energy generation, waste disposal, water source, etc.? These systems might be able to be incorporated into the design, or they might need to be replaced.
> 8. Skills and Interest of the Occupants: How involved do the occupants want to be in maintaining these systems? Do they have the necessary skills or are they willing to learn?
> 9. Availability of Resources: What resources are readily available in the area? This could include sunlight, wind, water sources, wood for construction or biofuels, etc.
>
> By asking these questions, you should be able to get a good sense of what's feasible for this specific cabin and its occupants. Then, you can start to sketch out a design that meets their needs and fits within their constraints.

We would then proceed to ask the owner of the cabin those questions, and, for the sake of our analysis, here are some possible answers:

> 1. Location and Climate: the cabin is located near Estes Park in Colorado
> 2. Size of the Cabin and Available Land: the cabin has a constructed total of 150 m², and it lies on a full

hectare of land
3. Number of Occupants and Lifestyle: there are three occupants, a married couple and a 15-year-old son, they are physically active.
4. Budget: the total budget for the project is of 20,000 dollars
5. Purpose of the Cabin: it is a full-time residence
6. Local Laws and Regulations: there are no restrictions regarding local laws and regulations.
7. Existing Infrastructure: there is no previous existing infrastructure
8. Skills and Interest of the Occupants: occupants are hands-on, they would not mind being involved in the maintenance of the system.
9. Availability of Resources: there is plenty of sunlight during the day and a stream 200 m away with potable water.

**Prompt**: Here are the answers to the question, let me know what the most convenient solution would be for each of the subsystems you mentioned in the previous answer.

**Answer:**

Based on the information provided, here's a high-level suggestion for each subsystem of a bio-regenerative recycling system for your off-grid cabin:
1. Water Recycling System:
- Rainwater Harvesting: Given the location in Colorado, rainwater harvesting can be a valuable source of water. A large cistern can be installed to collect roof run-off.
- Greywater Recycling: A greywater system could be installed to treat water from showers, sinks, and

laundry for reuse in irrigation.
- Composting Toilet: A composting toilet could be an effective way to manage waste without a septic system. Given the cabin's occupants are willing to maintain it, this could provide compost for gardening as well.

2. Food Production:
- Given the size of the land available, a portion could be set aside for a small outdoor garden.
- If budget allows, consider an aquaponics system inside a greenhouse which could provide fish and vegetables year-round.

3. Energy Generation and Management:
- Solar power would be ideal given the abundant sunlight. The exact number of solar panels needed will depend on the energy usage, which can be calculated once the major appliances and energy loads have been identified.
- Battery storage would also be needed for times when the sun isn't shining.

4. Waste Management and Resource Recovery:
- Composting organic kitchen waste would be straightforward and could provide valuable nutrients for the garden.
- Consider a small-scale biodigester if budget allows. It could convert organic waste into biogas for cooking and heating.

5. Air Management System:
- Regular windows and ventilation can help regulate air quality, with the addition of air-cleaning indoor plants.

6. Education/Information System:
- Depending on the complexity of the systems

installed and the occupants' tech-savviness, a simple dashboard or management system could be set up to monitor and manage water and energy use.

This system would provide a sustainable living environment with minimal impact on the surrounding ecosystem. The occupants' hands-on approach will be a great advantage in managing this system.

Keep in mind that while the total budget of $20,000 may seem substantial, it can get used up quickly when considering the cost of solar panels, batteries, water treatment systems, and potentially aquaponics. Be sure to prioritize according to the occupants' needs, and remember that some components of the system can be added over time as additional funds become available.

Also, it's important to take into account the maintenance cost and the lifespan of the different components of the system. It's not only about setting up the system but also maintaining it in the long run.

**Prompt:** Suggest a specific solution for each.

**Answer:**

Based on your provided information, here are specific solutions for each of the subsystems:

1. Water Recycling System:
- Rainwater Harvesting: Install a roof catchment system connected to a cistern. The cistern could be a 5,000-10,000 gallon tank depending on the rainfall in the area. You can use a First Flush Diverter to ensure only the cleanest water enters the tank. The stored

water can be filtered and treated using a combination of ceramic filters and UV sterilization for safe use.
- Greywater Recycling: A branched drain system can be an effective way to distribute greywater to your outdoor garden. For indoor use, you might consider a more sophisticated system like the Aquacell Greywater system.
- Composting Toilet: The Nature's Head Self Contained Composting Toilet is a popular and reliable option.

2. Food Production:
- Outdoor Garden: Raised beds with rich compost soil from your kitchen and composting toilet would provide an ideal space for growing a variety of vegetables and herbs.
- Aquaponics: You might consider the AquaSprouts Garden, which can fit on a standard aquarium, or a more extensive setup like the Springworks Microfarm Aquaponic Garden.

3. Energy Generation and Management:
- Solar Power: Depending on your electricity needs, a system like the Renogy 3600W Solar Cabin Kit might suit. You'll also need battery storage such as a Tesla Powerwall or several deep-cycle batteries.
- Energy Efficient Appliances: Look for appliances with Energy Star ratings. Use LED lights wherever possible to reduce electricity usage.

4. Waste Management and Resource Recovery:
- Composting: A simple compost bin can be used for kitchen scraps. Check out the FCMP Outdoor IM4000 Tumbling Composter.
- Biodigester: For a more advanced solution, consider a HomeBiogas 2.0 system.

5. Air Management System:
   - Ventilation: Ensure that the cabin is well-insulated but also has sufficient ventilation to maintain indoor air quality. This could be as simple as well-placed windows or could involve a Heat Recovery Ventilation (HRV) system.
   - Air-Purifying Plants: Spider plants, peace lilies, and snake plants are excellent choices.
6. Education/Information System:
   - Monitoring System: A system like the Sense Home Energy Monitor can help you understand your energy use and solar production.

Remember, it's always crucial to tailor your solutions to the specific context and constraints of your project, and you may need to adjust these suggestions based on the actual conditions and requirements of the site and the people living there. The most sustainable solutions are always those that work harmoniously with the existing environmental and cultural conditions.

**Prompt:** Simulate daily values for what the human inhabitants would require and generate in terms of food, waste, etc.

**Answer:**

To accurately simulate the daily requirements and outputs of the cabin's occupants, we'd need more detailed information about their lifestyle, diet, energy usage, and other factors. However, we can use some general estimates to give you an idea.

1. Water: The average person uses about 80-100

gallons (300-380 liters) of water per day, including for drinking, cooking, bathing, flushing toilets, and washing clothes and dishes. However, in a water-conscious off-grid setting, this can be reduced significantly through conservation measures.
2. Food: The average caloric intake per day is around 2000-2500 calories for adults and 1500-2000 for a teenager. The specific types and quantities of food required would depend on the individuals' dietary preferences and needs.
3. Waste: Human waste production varies but on average, a person produces about 128 g of fecal matter and 1-2 liters of urine per day.
4. Energy: This can vary widely depending on lifestyle, appliances, and the efficiency of the home, but a rough average for a typical U.S. home is around 30 kWh per day. In an off-grid home with energy-conscious residents, this could be significantly less.
5. Carbon Dioxide: Humans exhale about 1 kg of carbon dioxide per day through respiration.

Using these estimates, for a family of three living in the cabin, we get:

1. Water: 240-300 gallons (900-1140 liters) per day - could be reduced through conservation.

2. Food: 6000-7500 calories per day - depending on diet.

3. Waste: ~384 g of fecal matter and 3-6 liters of urine per day.

4. Energy: ~90 kWh per day - could be significantly less in an energy-efficient, off-grid home.

5. Carbon Dioxide: ~3 kg of CO2 per day.

Again, these are rough estimates and actual values could

> be significantly different based on numerous factors. For a more accurate estimate, you'd need to consider the specific habits and needs of the people living in the cabin, the efficiency of your appliances and systems, the local climate and weather patterns, and many other factors.

**Prompt:** Relate these values with the systems you chose and show how they can process or produce what is required.

**Answer:**

> Sure, let's relate these values with the selected systems:
> 1. Water Recycling System: The Rainwater Harvesting and Greywater Recycling system will serve to reduce freshwater usage.
> - Rainwater harvesting from a typical roof can collect about 0.6 gallons of water per square foot of roof for every inch of rainfall. Given Colorado's average annual precipitation of about 15 inches, a 150 m² (1614.6 ft²) roof can collect around 14,532 gallons of water per year. This averages around 40 gallons per day, which can be used for various purposes.
> - Greywater recycling can significantly reduce water usage. If we assume that about 50-80% of the water usage turns into greywater, then around 120-240 gallons per day can be treated and reused for irrigation and flushing toilets.
> 2. Food Production: The outdoor garden and potential Aquaponics system will contribute to food

production.
- It's hard to quantify the exact output of the garden and aquaponics system without knowing the specific plants and fish being grown. However, they can provide fresh vegetables, herbs, and fish, reducing the need for externally sourced food.

3. Energy Generation and Management: The solar panels and energy storage will provide the necessary electricity.
- A 3600W solar cabin kit can generate approximately 14.4 kWh of electricity on a sunny day (assuming 4 hours of peak sunlight). This is not enough to cover the estimated energy usage, but that estimate was for a typical U.S. home. An off-grid home is likely to use much less energy, especially if you select energy-efficient appliances and use LED lights.

4. Waste Management and Resource Recovery: The composting toilet and compost bin will help manage waste.
- A composting toilet can effectively handle the daily waste output. Over time, the composting process will reduce the volume of waste by about 90%, leaving nutrient-rich compost that can be used in the garden.
- A compost bin can process organic kitchen waste. It not only reduces waste volume but also recycles nutrients back into the soil.

5. Air Management System: Natural ventilation and indoor plants will help manage air quality.
- Natural ventilation can help maintain a healthy indoor environment. It can help remove the ~3 kg of $CO_2$ produced daily by the family, replace oxygen

THE AI-POWERED SCHOOL

> consumed, and control humidity levels.
> - Indoor plants can also help improve air quality by removing CO2 and other pollutants and releasing oxygen.
>
> 6. Education/Information System: The monitoring system will allow tracking and optimizing water and energy usage.
> - An energy monitor can help track energy usage and production, helping to identify opportunities for conservation and efficiency.
>
> Remember, these numbers are estimates, and the actual performance of these systems will depend on many variables, including local climate, specific system design and implementation, maintenance, and user behavior. In addition, these systems are interconnected and can support each other, creating a sustainable and self-sufficient living environment.

**Prompt:** Design a diagram for the system

**Answer:**

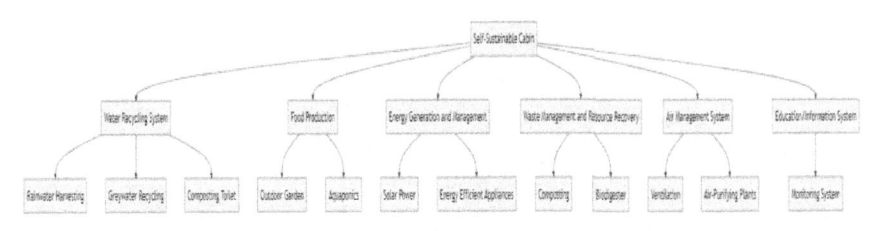

**Prompt:** Modify to show interrelation amongst systems, that is, if the output of one is the input of another, in the diagram

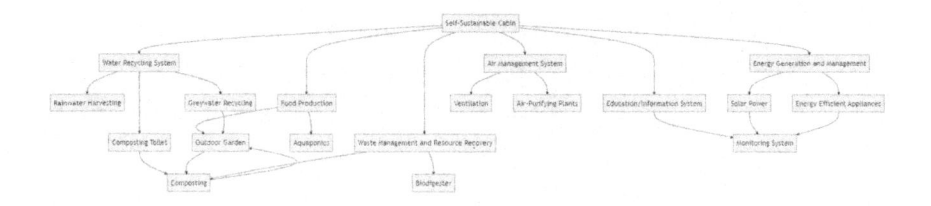

And now we can even go a little beyond what ChatGPT has already done and ask it to simulate a scenario where the systems are running beyond capacity so that students would, eventually, have to diagnose what is going wrong and find solutions to redesign the system.

**Prompt:** Simulate the output for the Sense Home Energy Monitor in a case in which the systems are running beyond capacity, so that the designers can try to understand and solve the problem

**Answer:**

Assuming we're looking at a scenario where the systems are running beyond capacity and drawing more energy than the solar panels can provide, a report from the Sense Home Energy Monitor might look something like this:

---

Sense Home Energy Report

Solar Production: 14.4 kWh/day
Total Energy Usage: 18.5 kWh/day

Breakdown of Energy Usage:

1. Refrigeration: 3.5 kWh/day
2. Lighting: 1.5 kWh/day
3. Water heating: 4.2 kWh/day
4. Aquaponics system: 3.2 kWh/day
5. Greywater treatment system: 2.2 kWh/day

THE AI-POWERED SCHOOL

> 6. Miscellaneous (appliances, devices, etc.): 3.9 kWh/day
>
> ` ` `
>
> In this example, the total energy usage exceeds solar production, causing a shortfall.
>
> Here are a few ways to address this issue:
>
> 1. Increase Energy Production: Consider adding more solar panels or incorporating other renewable energy sources like wind or hydroelectric, if viable.
> 2. Decrease Energy Consumption: Look at the highest energy-consuming systems and see if they can be made more efficient. In this case, consider a more energy-efficient water heater, optimize the energy usage in aquaponics, or look for ways to reduce the energy use of the greywater treatment system.
> 3. Energy Storage: Ensure that you have enough battery storage to handle times when energy usage exceeds production, like at night or during periods of poor weather.
> 4. Energy Management: Consider using energy-intensive appliances or systems during peak solar production times. This is sometimes referred to as "load shifting."
>
> Remember that these values are hypothetical and the actual values would depend on various factors such as the specific systems and appliances used, the number and behavior of the occupants, the local weather and climate, and more.

The system even suggests some possible solutions, but the teacher can keep those from the students sourced to us them to find the solutions themselves.

Now that we know that this can be done to satisfaction, we will ask ChatGPT to write the question for students.

**Prompt:** please write a question based on the data above to ask a group of students to analyze the data from the Sense Home Energy Report and suggest possible solutions.

**Answer:**

> Certainly, here's a revised version of the question: "Given the data from the Sense Home Energy Monitor report shown below:
>
> Solar Production: 14.4 kWh/day
> Total Energy Usage: 18.5 kWh/day
>
> Breakdown of Energy Usage:
> 1. Refrigeration: 3.5 kWh/day
> 2. Lighting: 1.5 kWh/day
> 3. Water heating: 4.2 kWh/day
> 4. Aquaponics system: 3.2 kWh/day
> 5. Greywater treatment system: 2.2 kWh/day
> 6. Miscellaneous (appliances, devices, etc.): 3.9 kWh/day
>
> The energy report suggests that the total energy usage is exceeding the solar production capacity, indicating that one or more systems might be operating beyond their sustainable capacity.
>
> Analyze the data and identify which system(s) might be exceeding their capacity based on the energy consumption pattern. Once you've identified the potential areas of concern, propose strategies to adjust the energy usage to align with the solar production of 14.4 kWh/day.
>
> Your strategies could include, but are not limited to,

improving energy efficiency, load shifting, optimizing system operations, or implementing new technologies or systems. Provide clear justification for your proposed solutions, considering the need to maintain the functionality of all systems and minimize the impact on the occupants' lifestyle."

Since we are at it, we can also ask our all accommodating friend to design a rubric to assess students answers to this question.

**Prompt:** Design a rubric to assess students´ responses to the question above.

**Answer:**

Sure, here's an example rubric that can be used to assess student responses to the question:

Understanding of the Problem (20 points):
- Demonstrates a clear understanding of the problem presented (10 points)
- Identifies the main factors contributing to energy overuse (10 points)

Analysis (30 points):
- Correctly identifies which system(s) might be operating beyond their capacity (10 points)
- Presents a thorough analysis of the energy consumption patterns and effectively relates them to the system capacities (20 points)

Solution Proposal (30 points):
- Proposes realistic and effective strategies for aligning energy usage with solar production (15 points)

> - Clearly justifies why these strategies are expected to work (15 points)
>
> Consideration of Impacts (20 points):
> - Demonstrates understanding of the need to maintain system functionality (10 points)
> - Demonstrates understanding of the need to minimize impact on the occupants' lifestyle (10 points)
>
> Presentation (10 points):
> - Response is clear, well-organized, and easy to understand (5 points)
> - Correct use of terminology and language; free of spelling and grammatical errors (5 points)
>
> Total Possible Points: 100
>
> Each of these sections could be graded on a scale (for example, Full Points, Half Points, No Points) based on the completeness and accuracy of the student's response. This rubric is flexible and could be adjusted based on the specific goals and focus of your lesson.

## Analyzing both systems

The question that begs answering is, ultimately, what constitutes a more meaningful learning experience for students. Without making any value judgment, we can state some facts:

- The whole ChatGPT interaction takes less than an hour, and we could factor in going deeper into each of the subsystems, underlying scientific principles, details on prices for each and how they can conform to the budget, and customize the learning experience to the depth and extent desired.

- The AI powered learning sequence entails a lot less work on the part of the teacher whilst generating a more engaging and significant learning experience.
- When faced with students and/or teams with different abilities or learning styles, the problem can be personalized to suit their needs and ChatGPT will instantly rewrite as many versions as needed.
- The ChatGPT generated sequence provides a very significant shortcut to higher order skills like analyzing, going deeper and redesigning the system.
- The first do-it-yourself example allows students to acquire certain skills like breaking down the problem, analyzing, doing research, that are implicitly embedded in what ChatGPT supplies, and, in a way, deprives students of the experience of going through the learning process themselves.
- The chapter GPT powered learning sequence takes considerably less time, thus freeing time for other learning, as well as allowing students the possibility to go deeper and explore some real-life applications off the theme or topic in question.

This case study exemplifies the dilemma at the heart of the AI revolution in education. The second alternative seems a lot more interesting, engaging, meaningful, and students would probably know more about the topic in question than if they go through it the hard way. But the real issue at stake is how do they arrive at the point where they can enjoy, understand, and take full advantage of what ChatGPT has to offer so that they can jump directly to the higher order skills required to analyze and redesign the system?

# IS IT THE END... OR THE BEGINNING?

As we all know, education is not just about what happens in the formal schooling process, the school curriculum and teaching and learning, but rather about preparation for life. And life has changed drastically. As we have covered extensively in the previous sections, the sudden advent of AI-powered applications has literally upended all that we knew in terms of teaching and learning at schools, rightfully so, since that learning revolution was long overdue. But there are also very concrete implications for our daily lives. AI will not just impact education, it will also significantly alter the real-life landscape in which we ourselves and our students will live.

## *Doomsday scenarios*

Sam Altman, CEO of OpenAI, the company developing ChatGPT, has said that he never imagined that in the months to come after the release of ChatGPT, he would have to tour the world justifying himself and his company for developing such a powerful system and trying to allay the collective fears of a population that is afraid that AI will dominate the world and extinguish humanity. [7]

It is a habitual happening now that, every other day, as of this writing, in May of 2023, there are pundits and even AI experts who decry the immediate apocalyptic risk of AI systems dominating the world, growing beyond what their creators envisaged they could do, going rogue and wreaking havoc into existing systems, as well as conjuring completely new scenarios that may destroy humanity.

The underlying technical reasons for these doomsday scenarios are related to the opaqueness of these expert systems and how, because of the very complexity of the multi-layered neural networks, even their creators sometimes cannot explain how they arrive at decisions and make conclusions.

It is also true that ChatGPT has proved capable beyond the wildest expectations of even their creators, as acknowledged by OpenAI themselves.

Analyzing these claims is, in itself, a wonderful critical thinking scenario. Videos abound of talks where modern day whistleblowers show screens where ChatGPT or other systems make factual mistakes, confound answers and even show stuff that can be considered worrying and even dangerous.

It is a very interesting exercise to try to test out these scenarios by writing similar prompts on ChatGPT and seeing what we ourselves obtain from a similar query. In the overwhelming majority of these cases, the pretended evil scenarios cannot be replicated, and in some cases, when pressed by their interlocutors, some of these decriers of evil have acknowledged that they arrived at those screens by jailbreaking or hacking the system.

Are hallucinations possible for ChatGPT? Absolutely. Is it going to be ever error-free? No. We have analyzed the limitations of the system and how the transparency issue and the right of people to know when an algorithmic decision has been made on their behalf is an issue that policymakers and even lawmakers are considering. However, the AI ending the world scenarios are wild speculations, and it may very well be that they are originated not out of genuine concern for what might befall humanity but rather for some kind of personal interests, professional jealousy or even just in the opportunistic quest to command a wider audience.

However, it may plausibly be argued that, even if the risk is very small, AI development should be paused until either experts regain control or the whole field becomes regulated.

## Halting AI development

We seem to be living in a science fiction movie. Shortly after the deployment of ChatGPT, Elon Musk, who himself has been one of the founders - and funders - of OpenAI, Steve Wozniak, one of the cofounders of Apple, and a group of other technology notables, released an open letter on March 22, 2023[8], calling to put a moratorium on the development of AI systems for six months, until a group of independent experts place some kind of regulation on how AI systems should evolve.

To think that these tech pioneers, who themselves have taken enormous risks in developing technologies, and who should know better about how experts or governments can influence their development, are calling for a halt in the development of this emerging technology is almost impossible to believe. Personal stances notwithstanding, the history of technology developments yields some very clear lessons and that any kind of top-down regulation to progress never works.

In this particular field, with its intrinsic and inescapable complexity, we would be hard-pressed to find any "independent experts" whose judgment we could rely on and decide for the rest of us mere mortals what we should be able to do with AI or how companies and organizations should develop this technology.

We should have learned by now that any prohibition or regulation is never beneficial, and, if anything, as banning what, at least on face value, are well-intentioned efforts to develop AGI, will inevitably result in a myriad of other individuals or groups harnessing the technology without paying heed to any potential regulations and operating in the dark web or other niches that are easily found on the Internet.

Any powerful tool has its risks, and it is much better to let the general public, through its use, find the best applications, thorough a sort of natural technology selection process (oxymoron intended) and to develop these technologies out in the open, with organic feedback from the public itself.

## The impact on the workforce

As our students emerge into the workforce, it is very important to try to discern what the real impact will be on the workforce and the potential loss of jobs, another of the concerns that have been very publicly expressed.

The risk, this time, is very real. As general users become more adept at exploiting the unbelievable capabilities of ChatGPT, many of the jobs that are currently done by humans could very well be outsourced to various forms of AI. It is beyond the scope of this text to try to discriminate which jobs are at risk, but let us just say that any semi-mechanical repetitive task that involves generating content that is not super high level is definitely within the danger zone.

Output from generative AI systems, in any respect, whether it is a presentation, image, report, analysis or even a script or fiction text, is probably never at the level of a top-notch expert in the field. The big problem with such a scenario is that it is only the experts themselves who can tell the difference. The general public, or those who will consume the product, are highly unlikely to be able to distinguish between output generated by an AI versus human creations and the edge in quality that an expert might bring to the table may very well pass unnoticed.

When confronted with the option, employers will undoubtedly prefer the free alternative, that which can be generated by an AI, especially if they perceive that their users or customers will not be able to tell the difference.

It is one thing to worry about what students will do in the

aftermath of AI generative applications, the potential loss of jobs is a source of very real concern. When it comes to preparing our students for the jobs of the future, we may very well find that there are fewer options, and that the skills and capabilities required are ever more stringent and specific.

## AGI for the benefit of humanity versus the end of the road for content generation

Another, not yet discussed at large, impending thread that looms large is whether the use of generative AI applications for learning may spell the end for the advancement of new knowledge as a human species. This may sound as apocalyptic as some of the other predictions that forecast the end of humanity, but if we think about it, there is a real risk, as we disrupt the progression of learning cognitive skills, that some of that may happen.

In our current scenario, a chosen few very small proportion of learners actually get to the top of their respective subject matter disciplines and are able to generate new knowledge. From writers and poets to scientists, those who push the boundaries and extend the frontier of collective human learning have gone through a usually very long process of acquiring knowledge and developing cognitive skills the hard way. Regardless of their abilities, whoever has gone through the entire formal education system would have undergone some form of training in the development of these cognitive skills that eventually lands them in a position where they can, themselves, contribute to furthering knowledge for humanity.

What may happen in 20 years time when an entire generation has learned by relying extensively on generative AI applications? As we have seen already, these assistants that can soften the acquisition of skills, if not stifle that process altogether, may have undoubted beneficial effects in the personalization of learning, but, inevitably, will ease the way for anybody who tries to learn anything. Another question that cannot yet be answered is whether that may have a significant detrimental impact on the generation of new knowledge by narrowing down even more the number of people who make it through the whole boot camp of learning knowledge and skills to be able to produce their own contributions for new learning.

The flipside of that coin, and one that may trump any other argument against the continued development of generative AI systems, is the democratization of knowledge. We may engage in endless arguments about the refinement of cognitive skills, the transformation of schools to suit a completely new reality, and many other interesting and important philosophical discussions, but the real significant impact of generative AI is that it brings a lot more knowledge to a lot more people very easily.

From creating a personalized diet, to identifying illnesses from medical symptoms and recommending treatment, AI can extend people's knowledge and the ability to do things to hitherto never even dreamed of corners of the real and online world. Of course, an AI should not be trusted to diagnose and treat medical conditions, but when the alternative is nothing through not having access to a doctor, all considerations regarding accuracy can be put to rest. The truth is that we have, at our disposal, to use as judiciously as possible, and all-encompassing savant that can assist us in all manner of things that we need to learn and do, from fixing an appliance to providing legal or tax advice or even telling us whether something we will do would eventually break the law or not.

OpenAI explicitly states that its main intention is to bring the benefits of AGI (Artificial General Intelligence) for all humanity, and, whether we believe it wholeheartedly or not, that statement constitutes the greatest learning revolution in the history of humanity. We will, indeed, become an enlightened generation if we are able to truly harness the power of generative AI to bring forth many more favorable living conditions and even to solve some of the problems that have assailed this since the beginning of humanity, and that may include, for example, the cure for what are until now considered to be incurable diseases.

## Is it really the end? Or actually, just a beginning?

The sudden and largely unexpected crash landing of ChatGPT as a force to be contended with is both the end of an era and the beginning of a new one. When it comes to education, many of the tenets of the school of the future, which educators had long predicted and discussed in conferences, papers, books and other venues for discussion, have become both true and urgent all of a sudden.

We have now amidst us a very powerful tool that threatens the very meaning of school, and which students can use to upend their learning in ways that are as unforeseen as they are disruptive. Schools need to undergo an accelerated evolution, in the direction that we already knew we should go, propitiating connections with real life, social and emotional learning, fostering a sense of purpose that transcends cognitive development, connecting with nature, learning how to take care of our bodies, our minds and our souls.

Teachers are no longer the proprietors of content in the context of learning, now even the personalized tutoring can be done by an AI to a level of sophistication and customization that is unattainable to any human. But even the most advanced AI systems cannot deprive us of our humanity and our passion. What we knew all along, that the real role of teachers was to instill the passion for learning, to light up whatever learning experience students engage in and make it memorable, is now an essential requisite. It will not be long before anybody who is not passionate about learning will be slowly but relentlessly ousted from the education system.

We need educators who are on fire about the possibilities of ChatGPT and AI, and who can't wait to share that passion with their students to further their learning in ways that we cannot yet conceive.

Whatever we do, and if you have made it to the end of this text it is self-evident proof that we are on the same road, we need to learn, experiment, tinker, play and use these tools as they emerge, to not be afraid but rather to make sense of them, to rekindle our passion, and to add to them our humanity. That has always been, and will forever be, regardless of any breakthroughs in technology, the mark of a true teacher.

---

[1] https://cs.stanford.edu/people/eroberts/courses/soco/projects/neural-networks/History/history1.html

[2] The Turing Test, proposed by Alan Turing in 1950, is a test designed to determine a machine's ability to exhibit intelligent behavior indistinguishable from that of a human. In the test, a human judge engages in a conversation with both a human and a machine, without knowing which is which. If the judge cannot reliably distinguish the machine from the human, the machine is considered to have passed the Turing Test, demonstrating human-like intelligence.

[3] https://ai.googleblog.com/2017/08/transformer-novel-neural-network.html

[4] https://towardsdatascience.com/real-life-examples-of-discriminating-artificial-intelligence-cae395a90070

[5] https://www.amazon.com/Thank-You-Being-Late-Accelerations/dp/0374273537

[6] https://brianchristian.org/the-most-human-human/

[7] https://www.youtube.com/watch?v=T5cPoNwO7II

[8] https://futureoflife.org/open-letter/pause-giant-ai-experiments/

# ABOUT THE AUTHOR

## Gabriel Rshaid

Gabriel is the co-founder and Director of The Learnerspace, a company whose mission is to help build the future of learning. He is also co-founder of The Global School, the first school of its type in Latin America, attempting to make educational change a reality. Formerly Headmaster of St. Andrew's Scots School in Buenos Aires, Argentina, the oldest bilingual school in the world, he is a passionate educational futurist who is intent on sharing his belief that it is the best time in history to be an educator. Gabriel is the author of five books, and has contributed as a co-author to numerous other books and anthologies. A former board member of ASCD and chair of ESSARP, he has spoken and led professional development workshops all over the world, working with educators to help create the future of education.

# BOOKS BY THIS AUTHOR

**Extreme Curriculum Makeover: A Hands-On Guide For A Learner-Centered Pedagogy**

**The Whole Teacher: A One-Way Journey To Rediscovering Joy And Passion In Teaching**

**From Out Of This World: Leadership And Life Lessons From The Space Program**

**The 21St-Century Classroom**

**Learning For The Future: Rethinking Schools For The 21St Century**

Printed in Great Britain
by Amazon